TOTAL
SURRENDER

DESIRES
INCLUDED

DEBRA OLSON BRAGA

TATE PUBLISHING
AND ENTERPRISES, LLC

Published by Tate Publishing & Enterprises, LLC
127 E. Trade Center Terrace | Mustang, Oklahoma 73064 USA
1.888.361.9473 | www.tatepublishing.com

Tate Publishing is committed to excellence in the publishing industry. The company reflects the philosophy established by the founders, based on Psalm 68:11,
"The Lord gave the word and great was the company of those who published it."

Book design copyright © 2011 by Tate Publishing, LLC. All rights reserved.
Cover design by Kristen Verser
Interior design by April Marciszewski

Published in the United States of America

ISBN: 978-1-61346-685-8
Religion / Christian Life / Spiritual Growth
11.10.10

DEDICATION

To my husband and best friend, Joe.

To my four wonderful children, who encouraged me to write this book. Thank you, Julie, Jennifer, David, and Jessica.

To my Christian parents, Bob and Mary Olson, and my sisters, Linda, Vanessa, and to Wanda (who went to be with the LORD).

To my intercessors and friends: Shirley, Miriam, Sylvia, Kathy, and Leah. You all have been lifesavers—literally!

To Marilyn, a pastor's wife who changed my life. To Donna and Scott, who continued the work that Marilyn started! Thank you.

TOTAL
SURRENDER

CONTENTS

INTRODUCTION

The Bible says to "Seek ye first the kingdom of God, and His righteousness; and all these things shall be added unto you" (Matthew 6:33). The church has spent too much of its time on what "shall be added unto you." How do we know what should "be added" unto us if we don't know His will for our life? If we spent more time seeking *His* will and *His* ways, everything else would follow. I challenge you to totally surrender to Him. There isn't anything you can't trust Him with. Many people "accept the LORD" by going through the sinner's prayer, but since they never submit their will and desires to the LORD, they don't end up walking with the LORD, or they don't ever grow into a mature believer. If you are struggling with your walk with God, this might be the reason for your difficulties. When we accept the LORD, we need to turn our *entire* life over to Him.

Matthew 7:8–11 says,

> For every one that asketh receiveth; and he that seeketh findeth; and to him that knocketh it shall be opened. Or what man is there of you whom if his son ask bread, will he give him a stone? Or if he ask a fish, will he give him a serpent? If ye then, being evil, know how to give good gifts unto your children, how much more shall your Father which is in heaven give good things to them that ask him?

This scripture not only points out that we can trust God with our lives and desires, but it makes a point that when we seek Him, we will find Him. Sometimes we are just not asking. Sometimes we are not seeking Him. Many people are spending too much time seeking what they can get from Him. It doesn't say that we will find Him if we seek material possessions. We must *seek Him first*. We must choose to let the LORD mold our lives and desires into what He wants them to be.

James 4:7–8 says, "Submit yourselves therefore to God. Resist the devil, and he will flee from you. Draw nigh to God, and He will draw nigh to you. Cleanse your hands, ye sinners; and purify your hearts, ye doubleminded." Verse 10 says, "Humble yourselves in the sight of the LORD, and He shall lift you up."

Submit to Him. Draw close to Him. This scripture talks about being cleansed and purified. This is done by drawing close to God and staying there. I challenge you to do this while reading this book. Read a chapter and then put on a praise-and-worship CD and spend time soaking in His presence. Start with ten minutes a day. I personally recommend at least thirty minutes. When possible, I suggest that you spend at least two hours with the LORD. It may sound overwhelming. Please, just make a commitment to spend time with Him.

In Deuteronomy 18, God says that when He chooses someone to minister before Him, they must "come with all the desire of his mind unto the place which the LORD shall choose." Please note that we must come before Him with *all* the desires of our mind. First Timothy 1:12 says, "And I thank Christ Jesus our LORD, who hath enabled me, for that He counted me faithful, putting me into the ministry." Do you want to be used by God? There is no better place to be in this world than the place that God chooses for us. Let God reposition you to where He wants you. Let God reveal His plan for your life. When you have let the LORD do this in your life, you can then rest in the peace of knowing that you have put the LORD where He wants to be in your life.

Deuteronomy 13:3–4 says that God has to prove us to know whether or not we love the LORD with all of our heart and soul. We must walk after God, fear Him (a reverence and respect for Him), keep His commandments, obey His voice, serve Him, and *cleave* to Him. We cannot expect God's blessings in our lives unless we do all of these things. Do we really *cleave* to Him? We have to honestly ask ourselves this question. We all need to repent if we don't. Romans 13:14 says that we are to not make provision for our flesh. This means that we are not to let our flesh rule us. We are not supposed to feed the flesh either. We are to crucify the flesh and cleave to Him.

> And all Judah rejoiced at the oath: for they had sworn with all their heart, and *sought Him with their whole desire*; and He was found of them: and *the* LORD *gave them rest round about.*
>
> 2 Chronicles 15:15 (emphasis mine)

In other words, Judah sought Him with all their desires and with their entire heart, and they found Him. The LORD awarded them with peace and rest.

I have seen countless lives destroyed because they could not submit their desires to the LORD. I have seen people end up totally in the wrong place and married to the wrong people because they chased after personal desires that were not submitted to the LORD. I had a young lady ask me why God made her marry such a terrible person. I asked her, "How did God make you get married?" She could not come up with an answer. Finally, I asked her one simple question, "Did you ask God if you should marry that man?" She finally admitted that she just assumed that he was the right one.

It is a question of trust. We can trust Him totally and completely. In the Bible, we have a classic example of this.

Sarah knew that her husband, Abraham, had heard from the LORD, but she didn't trust the LORD to fulfill that promise by Himself. So she thought that she would help God out. Of course, that lead to nothing but trouble.

In this book, I hope to share with you some of my testimony of how incredible my life has been following these simple truths. I hope the stories included here will help build your faith—faith for healing, finances, signs and wonders, and everything else that the LORD wants to bless you with. As you read each story, I would hope that you would pray and ask the LORD to help you to trust Him with all aspects of your life. I have spent my life devoted to the LORD's plan for me and my family. I submitted my desires to the LORD as a teen and I continue to submit myself to Him. Pray the prayer, "LORD, I want to desire what You desire. I, of my own free will, ask You to take my desires and make them match Your desires. In Jesus' name, Amen."

There are scriptures included in the chapters. Please read each scripture. Ask the LORD to bring the message of each verse to life for you and to help you to understand it and see the Word the way that He wants for you to apply it to your life.

A HUMBLE BEGINNING

I was saved when I was five years old. I don't remember ever *not* serving the LORD. I spent a lot of time with my father. I could ask him any question, and he always had an answer from the Bible. He would not tell me what to believe. He would give me all the scripture references having to do with a topic and then let me read them and come to my own conclusions. It was an incredible way to learn the Word. Since I have raised four children now, I realize just how difficult it is not to just tell your kids what to believe. I also realize how marvelous it was to have a father who knew the Word that well. It really takes a lot of time in the Word to be able to remember all of the scriptures pertaining to everything—and he didn't need a concordance to do it. My father taught me that we are supposed to go to the Word to find out what to believe. People get off track when they decide to go to the Word to back up what they have decided that *they want* to believe. You can always pick out parts of verses to back up just about anything, but we are supposed to believe the entire Bible—not just bits and pieces.

I also remember hearing my father cry and pray for the Jewish people and Israel. I finally asked him, "Why do you spend so much time praying for the Jewish people and Israel?" He explained to me that the Jewish people are God's chosen people and that we must be willing to "take the shirt off our back," if necessary, to help the Jewish people. He showed me in the scriptures the truth of what God says. It is clear in the scriptures that God blesses those who bless Israel (the Jewish people) and curses those who curse Israel.

Genesis 12:3 says, "And I will bless them that bless thee, and curse him that curseth thee; and in thee shall all families of the earth be blessed."

When I was a teenager, I remember hearing a sermon on turning your heart completely over to the LORD. We are supposed to totally surrender to Him. One of the ways to do that was by praying and turning your desires over to Him. It is a simple prayer. I prayed a prayer that day that would change my life. I prayed, "LORD, I want to desire what You desire. I, of my own free will, ask You to take my desires and make them match Your desires." I challenge you to pray this prayer. First Peter 4:2 says that we are no longer supposed to live according to the lusts of man, but we are supposed to live according to the "will of God." When you totally submit your desires to Him, joy will come deep in your heart when you do what He asks you to do.

I have heard many people say that they are "scared" that God will make them do something that they do not want to do—like go to Africa. We do not need to start out with going to Africa. (I have friends that are missionaries to Africa, and they believe that Africa is wonderful.) When you start out with the simple truth, the simple prayer, "Make my desires match Your desires," He will take care of the rest. You will enjoy your life. I have been asked many times over the years, "How do I know God's will for my life?" When you pray and turn your desires over to Him, it becomes a lot easier to know His will. When Jesus told us how to pray, it was really clear that we are supposed to be praying for *His will* to be done. It doesn't say anywhere in the prayer that we are supposed to pray for *our* will or desires.

"Thy kingdom come, Thy will be done in earth, as it is in heaven" (Matthew 6:10).

"… Not as I will, but as Thou wilt" (Matthew 26:39).

Philippians 2:8 tells us that Jesus even humbled Himself and was obedient to the will of the Father—even to death on the cross.

I graduated from high school and went to college in Minnesota. I met Joe there. Joe came to me one day soon after our engagement and told me that God had spoken to him and told him to devote his life to the Jewish people and their well being. I said, "Of course," and we made plans to get married.

We owed five hundred dollars on Joe's tuition bill. It had to be paid or he would not be allowed to graduate. The college gave him all the way up to the finals to pay the bill. Two weeks before the finals, we had one hundred dollars to put toward his bill, but the LORD spoke to Joe and told him to give that money away. We gave that money to the college's building project. One week before finals, the school sent out statements to all the students. Joe and I took his statement to the billing office. You see, his bill said "Balance paid in full." We asked them what had happened to the five hundred dollars that we owed. They informed us that the bill had been paid anonymously! This small miracle was only just the beginning of things to come. Joe took his finals and graduated. We got married in Ohio a week after that.

Joe told me a couple of days before the wedding that we would be moving to Israel some day. At the time, I had no desire in my heart to move to Israel. I knew that because I had prayed, "LORD, make my desires match Your desires!" that if I was going to live in Israel some day that my heart would change. My heart didn't change overnight, but it did change over time. I have visited Israel once and I now long to move there.

"Commit thy way unto the LORD; trust also in Him; and He shall bring it to pass" (Psalms 37:5).

Joe had taught me some things before we got married. One of the most important lessons was about taking the time to see others as He sees them. When I got to college,

I was an emotional mess. I had hypoglycemia and didn't know it, and that greatly affected the way that I responded to things. When Joe asked me to marry him, I asked him how he could want to marry me when I was such a mess. He replied, "I don't see you as a mess. I see you as a beautiful handmaiden of the LORD." I asked him how he could possibly see me that way. He replied, "I see you through the eyes of the LORD." I was so in love with him after that.

When you see someone filthy, in torn clothes, or acting strangely, ask the LORD to help you to see that person through *His* eyes. Then ask Him to show you what He wants you to do to show His love to that person. We need to make sure that we do what we know is right in the sight of the LORD and we know that He wants us to treat everyone with respect.

> But the LORD said unto Samuel, look not on his countenance, or on the height of his stature; because I have refused him: for the LORD seeth not as man seeth; for man looketh on the outward appearance, but the LORD looketh on the heart.
>
> 1 Samuel 16:7

The LORD says that if we do something for someone in need that we are doing it for Him and if we do not help them in need, we are neglecting Him as well. Matthew 25 says,

Verse 40: "…Inasmuch as ye *have done* it unto one of the least of these my brethren, ye *have done* it unto me."

Verse 45: "…In asmuch as did it *not* to one of the least of these, ye did it *not* to me."

NEVER SAY NEVER

My life since my wedding has been anything but normal. First of all, my aunt and uncle loaned us their pop-up-tent camper to use for our honeymoon, so we were able to travel over six thousand miles and take a thirty-five-day honeymoon, traveling across the northern US and through Canada on very little money.

While we were in Oregon, the Lord told a friend of ours, Larry, to give us tires for our car. The tires on our car were bald, and God took care of replacing them for us. We knew that He had provided us the camper and He would take care of everything else. It definitely was a gift from God.

After our honeymoon was over, we were invited by a pastor in Florida to move there, which we did. I had been to Florida as a teenager but didn't like it. I told God that I *never* wanted to live in Florida. Of course, I learned the important lesson of not saying *never* to the LORD but, "LORD, make my desires match Your desires." We lived in Florida for almost eighteen years.

DOCTORS ARE NOT INFALLIBLE

We started having our family immediately. In fact, we had our first child eleven months after we got married. We had only been in Florida for three months when she was born. When I was pregnant with her, I was experiencing symptoms that meant that it was a good chance that I was going to have a miscarriage. There was also someone in my life that was telling me that my baby was going to be miscarried.

I went to a ladies' luncheon at a conference that my husband and I were attending. I was put at a table sitting next to a woman that I did not know. I had never seen her before. I was only ten weeks pregnant, so no one at that point could tell that I was pregnant. While eating lunch, the woman turns to me and says, "The LORD told me that you are worried about losing this baby. He said not to worry. The scriptures say, 'The LORD will perfect that which concerneth me' (Psalms 138:8a). That means that the LORD will finish His work in this baby. You don't need to worry." So every time from that point on when the symptoms would come, my husband would lay his hands on my belly and would quote that verse. Julie was born full term and was born perfect.

The pregnancy and delivery of my second child two and a half years later went smoothly. When I had the blood work done on my third pregnancy, they found an antibody in my blood that was dangerous to the baby. I have negative blood and all of my children were born with positive blood. I had the shots, but antibodies still can form. They informed me that if the antibody crossed the placenta, it could harm or even kill the baby. They wanted to do an amniocentesis to see if the baby was okay. I wanted to know what they were going to do if they found the baby "under attack." They said that they would then counsel me to have an abortion. I told them no. I had a midwife program that included a doctor. The midwife suggested that we wait until the time of viability (seven months) before doing the amniocentesis. That way, if the amniocentesis showed the baby in danger, they could induce labor and the baby could be delivered and would survive. The doctor finally agreed to that. We reluctantly agreed.

I had the test done. The test results came back stating that the antibody had crossed the placenta and was starting to attack the baby. The doctor initially wanted me to consider letting him induce labor and have me give birth to my son two months early. I said no. He then wanted me to have an amniocentesis every two weeks to check the baby. I said no. I knew the baby was okay, and I wasn't going to let him touch me again. His office kept calling me and putting pressure on me. Every time we prayed about it, peace would come and we knew the baby would be okay.

In the meantime, the midwife had me counting baby movements for an hour every afternoon. The baby was moving over one hundred movements per hour. The doctor then told me that the baby would have to be taken by C-Section. He claimed that the baby was moving too much. He said that the baby was going to end up with the cord wrapped around his neck. He came up with every negative thing that he could think of. He never had anything positive to say. It was hard listening to him and not letting fear overtake me. Once again I used the scripture given to me in my first pregnancy. I stood on the Word that had been given to me years before.

Finally, the doctor told me that if I didn't have another amniocentesis by Monday, March 30, I would be kicked out of their care and I would be left without a physician. The midwife told me that she could not postpone it anymore. She scheduled me for an amniocentesis on Monday, March 30, 1987. I told her not to worry, because I would have the baby by then. By the way, my due date was April 11. I went into labor and had David on March 28, 1987. David weighed 8 pounds, 13 ounces and was twenty-three inches long. He was perfect. There was absolutely no sign of damage from the antibody or anything else. "The LORD will perfect that which concerneth me; thy mercy, O LORD, endureth forever…" (Psalms 138:8).

By the way, David was born naturally, but barely. They said that the umbilical cord was too short to have gotten wrapped around his neck. They said that he would have had to be taken by C-section if the cord were any shorter, because he would not have been able to get all the way out. God even had the umbilical cord covered.

I went in for my six-week post-baby check up, and the head midwife came in to see me. She told me that she had some strange news for me. You see, the amniotic fluid taken during an amniocentesis is always tested by two labs because of how important it is. The second lab had "lost" the test results. Two weeks *after* I had the baby, the lab found the results stuck in a corner under a desk. The lab then sent it to the doctor. The results were that the antibody had *not* crossed the placenta and that the baby was safe. It also makes you question the validity of some of the testing done. Why did the two labs give conflicting results? I believe it was a test to see what we would believe. Whose report are we supposed to believe?

We need to believe what the LORD tells us above anything being spoken to us by others.

During Julie's pregnancy, someone very close to me was telling me that I was going to have a miscarriage. During David's pregnancy, the doctor was telling me that David was going to die. In both cases, we chose to believe what the LORD said. In other words, we believed the report of the LORD.

I learned the importance of not letting negativity rule over me. I want you to make a list of things or people in your life that influence you to think and believe negatively. This can be very hard, but I ask you to pray and ask the LORD to remind you every time you are about to say something negative. We are allowed to ask for prayer if we need it, but there are positive ways to say things and negative ways to say things. We could say, "I am sick and tired of having these headaches. Please pray for me." But that isn't the way to say it. A better way to say it is, "I am trusting the LORD to heal me from having headaches. Please pray in agreement with me for that."

If there is someone in your life that is consistently talking defeat and negativity into your life, you may have to limit your contact with them until you are strong enough in this area. Ask the LORD to help you with the way that you talk about things and to help you to deal with the negative people in your life.

In Numbers 13, we have the story about the spies that were sent into the promised land. Half of them came back with a negative report and half of them came back with a positive report. It didn't go well for the ones that came back with the negative report. We need to pray and ask the LORD to show us how to look at things that are happening, and instead of seeing the negative, we need to see the potential that is there for good.

> Finally, brethren, whatsoever things are true, whatsoever things are honest, whatsoever things are just, whatsoever things are pure, whatsoever things are lovely, whatsoever things are of good report; if there be any virtue, and if there be any praise, think on these things.
>
> Philippians 4:8

WANT A HEALING? WILL YOU DO YOUR PART?

I did not feel well during most of my high school years. I would have sharp pains that would shoot through my head. I was hyperemotional. I could be crying one minute and laughing uncontrollably the next. The doctors that my parents took me to told me that I was born with a "lack of stamina." I was praying that the LORD would heal me or at least help us figure out what was going on. I also had a curvature in my back that caused me a lot of pain.

A member of the congregation that we attended in Florida was a chiropractor. He offered to treat my back for free, and of course, I couldn't say no to that. When I went to see him for the first time, he sat down with me to go over my health history. I told him all about the problems that I was having. When he took my blood pressure, he turned white as a sheet. He asked me to stand up, and he took my blood pressure again. This time, he sat down. He looked really upset, so I asked him what was wrong. He told me that my blood pressure sitting down was 50 over 40. He said that my blood pressure dropped even lower when standing up. He said that he would not give me those numbers because they were too terrible. He told me that I was hypoglycemic and that I could go and get more tests run by a medical doctor to get confirmation of that. He told me that he could offer me an herbal treatment program that would balance my system back out again. It was a costly program, and he said that he couldn't give it to me for free but that he would give it to me at his cost. I went home and discussed it with my husband. My friends asked me if I was going to ask the LORD to heal me. I told them that I wanted to get my appetite under control first. The chiropractor started me on the herbal program, and within three days, my blood pressure was stabilized to 100 over 70. I felt great. I stayed on the herbal treatment program for six months. It stabilized my appetite as well. I no longer craved sweets and sugar. I haven't had a problem since, and that was twenty-nine years ago! The chiropractor continued treating my back for a couple of years after that, but I never had to pray for healing of the hypoglycemia or blood pressure problems. They were gone. I believe that we need to be willing to do our part if we are asking the LORD for something. I have seen many people ask the LORD for things and then not take care of it. Sometimes they would get angry with God when things didn't work out.

I was at a meeting in another church, and the minister said that he wanted anyone that had back problems to come forward for prayer. My husband urged me to go up, so I did. The minister asked me what the problem was. I told him I couldn't remember the diagnosis but that my chiropractor was there. So the minister asked the chiropractor to come forward. The minister asked him what the diagnosis was, and he told him. The minister laid his hands on my back and prayed that everything would line up. My back snapped back in place, and my chiropractor passed out.

I believe that it is abusing the LORD's healing power to ask Him to heal you if you are not willing to do your part. I wasn't going to ask the LORD to heal me of hypoglycemia unless I had gotten my appetite under control. Unless you are willing to eat healthy, exercise, etc., in order to support the healing that you are asking for—do not ask the LORD to heal you. Part of submitting your desires to the LORD involves submitting to the fact that He wants us to live healthy, well-balanced lives.

The LORD will heal you. He will answer your prayers. It isn't a matter of that. I knew a man that was a friend of our family that had been healed of severe diabetes. The problem was that he did not change his eating habits. So he ended up eating himself right back into diabetes. He then spent hours upon hours crying out to the LORD to heal him again. I thought that it was crazy for him to expect that out of God. The Bible teaches us that faith without works is dead. Why should He heal us over and over again if we are not taking care of ourselves?

Are we taking His healing power and His answers to prayer for granted? What are you doing with the things that He has given you? I know that I get quite upset if I see one of my children mistreating something that I have given them. I have even had my children break things or lose things that I have given them because they were not careful. If I feel that way, I can only imagine how He feels.

James has a lot to say about this. James chapter two says:

Verse 14: "What doth it profit, my brethren, though a man say he hath faith, and have not works? Can faith save him?"

Verse 17: "Even so faith, if it hath not works, is dead, being alone."

Verse 20: "But wilt thou know, O vain man, that *faith without works is dead?*"

We are not saved by our works, but we are expected to work in cooperation with Him.

WARMING UP TO ISRAEL

When God spoke to my husband and told him that we would move to Israel some day, He told Joe that there would be three steps to the move. The first step was for Joe to go to Israel alone. In 1987, the LORD told us it was time for Joe to go. Joe was friends with a Rabbi who told him about a volunteer program where you can fly to Israel, stay three weeks, and fly back for a reduced cost. You do some kind of volunteer work five days a week and see the sights of Israel two days a week on special, military-escorted trips. We kept trying to raise the seven hundred dollars needed for the trip, but one deadline after another would pass for each trip.

We had four hundred dollars appear in our bank account in February of that year. I went to the bank and pointed out the error. They told me not to worry about it. They said that I must have made a mistake. We were not making enough money at that time for a four-hundred-dollar deposit to have been made into our account at one time. So I left the money in there for three months. I then went into the bank and had the bank manager go over my checkbook and transaction history with me. She told me that the money was ours. I clearly explained to her that it was a mistake, but she added the money to my checkbook balance and gave it back to me. I thanked her and left, praising God. All we are responsible to do is to be honest and bring other people's mistakes to their attention. I knew that I had done everything I could to rectify the situation. So, that money helped us to come up with the seven hundred needed for a flight leaving in July. We sent the money to the office in New York.

Three days before Joe left, we received a letter back from New York saying that a wealthy man from New York had picked the flight that Joe was going on and had decided to pay $350 of the cost for each person. So we got $350 back. It was amazing. Joe got to go to Israel, spend three weeks there, see the country, and return home for $350.

While he was in Israel, several things happened that helped him with spending money. The first thing that happened is that one of the other volunteers had found money on the sidewalk and decided to give it to Joe because, he said, he didn't need the money. The second thing that happened was that he was going through the old part of Jerusalem when an Arab gentleman started following him. He wanted to buy the watch that Joe had on. Joe told him that it wasn't worth anything, but he didn't want to sell it. The gentleman didn't believe him and demanded to pay ten dollars for it. Joe finally accepted the money and gave him the watch. You see, Joe had only paid three dollars for it a couple of months before the trip. The third thing that happened was that Joe had a Walkman. He had dropped it a couple of times, so it was cracked. Again, an Arab gentleman had demanded to buy it from him. He ended up paying Joe three times what it was worth, even though Joe told him that it wasn't worth that. By the way, by this time, my feelings for Israel had already started to turn.

If we give of ourselves and trust God to provide for us, He will. Even if you are not sure where the next dollar is coming from, be reassured that if you are doing *His will*, He will take care of you. It may come in some strange ways, as it did for Joe, but it will come. If you give everything to God, even what you think you don't have, God's grace will abound towards you.

GOD HAS A SENSE OF HUMOR

We went through a period of time when the children and my husband were frustrated about eating the same thing all the time. They were especially tired of eating ground meat. My husband really likes steaks, but we couldn't afford them at the time. I told them that if they wanted something different, they needed to pray about it. They did. I got called to work a temporary job selling meat at a department store. It was only for a week, for a special promotion that was going on.

At the end of the week, I was working the last shift of the sales event. The distributor came by and said that they could not ship any of the open boxes of meat back. He told us to split the open boxes between ourselves. It was amazing. We had all kinds of steaks and seafood, including T-bones, sirloins, NY strips, lobster, and shrimp. We had so much of it that it couldn't fit in our freezer. We had to store some of it in a neighbor's freezer, and we gave some away. My family got so tired of steaks that they asked me to stop making them. (Now, I don't want you to be tempted to grumble and complain so that the Lord will give you steaks and lobster to eat.)

The Lord will supply you with something different to eat from time to time if you live in an attitude of being appreciative. Ask the Lord to show you how to combine the foods that you have in your cupboard to make new things.

One day, I knew that I didn't have much food left in the cupboard and that we were not going to get paid until the next day. I opened up the cupboards and prayed, "Lord, please show me what I can make out of this." Sure enough, an idea came to me on how to turn what I had into a casserole. The things that I had in the cupboard were: 1. Three potatoes 2. A small chunk of cheese 3. A large can of tomato sauce 4. Chili powder. I took the potatoes and cheese and sliced them thin. I took the tomato sauce and put a small layer on the bottom of the casserole dish. I put a layer of potatoes on top of that, sprinkled chili powder on that layer, and then put a few pieces of cheese on top of that. I kept layering the potatoes, chili powder, cheese and tomato sauce. I made sure that there was cheese and tomato sauce on the top of the final layer. I covered it with aluminum foil and baked it. It was delicious. The interesting part of the story is that I tried to make the same thing later and it didn't taste as good. I truly believe that the LORD blessed it because I prayed over it.

"Giving thanks always for all things unto God and the Father in the Name of our LORD Jesus Christ" (Ephesians 5:20).

"For every one that asketh receiveth; and he that seeketh findeth; and to him that knocketh it shall be opened. Or what man is there of you, whom if his son ask bread, will he give him a stone? Or if he ask a fish, will he give him a serpent?" (Matthew 7:8–10).

God will give us good things if we ask. We need to make sure that we are asking Him for the right things. If you have anything that you really do need, bring your request before God first. Trust Him and He will provide for you.

Deuteronomy 8 tells us that God humbled the Israelites to prove them and to show what was deep in their hearts. He wanted to find out if they would obey His commandments. He had them eat manna so that they would learn that it is the words of the LORD that are important. Our family soon learned that it wasn't what you were eating that was important.

Several years later, we had ministers that were visiting our church come and stay with us. They were from Romania. They only drank water or milk. One day, they

asked us what we were drinking. We told them that it
was soda. They asked to have a small drink of it. We gave
them a glass full. They each took a couple of sips of the
drink. They then asked us, "What purpose does this serve
in your body?" We were surprised. We told them that
honestly there wasn't any. They then gave us back the rest
of the glass of soda. They said that they would not be
drinking any more of it. We felt quite convicted about
that. We didn't stop drinking soda, but we did cut back on
the amount that we drank.

Our children were on the free breakfast program at
their school. Every day they would come home and complain about what they were "forced" to eat for breakfast.
The Romanian couple got very sad listening to the children complain. Finally, they asked them what they were
being forced to eat. The children ran off the list of choices
(toast, eggs, cereal, etc.). The Romanian couple then
laughed. They told our children that their children are
fed only one thing for breakfast and then again for lunch
every day at school and that was plain oatmeal (no sugar
or anything) with a small amount of milk. Our children
did not complain again for over a year after that.

There was one other incident where my children was
asking me for one type of drink. The drink was expensive
at the time. So I simply told them that if they wanted
that to drink, that they needed to pray for it to go on sale
and/or for coupons to come out for it. Well, before long, I
noticed that the drink was on sale. The drink was on sale
for $1. I noticed that the label stated that there was a cou-
pon under the label for a $1 off of your next purchase. So

the second bottle was free. My kids got to drink the drink that they wanted for free all summer long.

They learned that lesson so well that they got together and talked about what their favorite cereal was. They agreed in prayer together, asking the LORD to supply that cereal. Sure enough, one particular store made a mistake in their ad for the week. They had this one cereal marked down to $2 per box and then in their ad, they had a coupon for $2 off per box. Of course, we stocked up. Yes, my children got to eat their cereal for free for quite a while. By the time the cereal was gone, my children were ready to eat something else anyway.

REALLY LISTEN

There was a couple that came from Israel to visit relatives in the States. Her parents had paid their way so that they could get to see them. Her parents did not attend our congregation, but the couple were friends with some of the people in our congregation. At that time, they were struggling to get by in Israel. A group of people from our congregation would get together and go out for coffee after service. We would invite this couple along, and we would all pitch in and treat them. We would ask them about what life was like in Israel. We had many wonderful discussions about it.

One of the things that they mentioned was that electric heat was way too expensive, so they pretty much lived without heat since they couldn't afford to pay for it. They told us that kerosene heat was the cheapest form of heat and that they were praying that the LORD would supply them with a kerosene heater.

The couple then left the area to see other relatives. They were gone for a couple of weeks. While they were gone, I couldn't get the whole thing out of my head. So I prayed about it. I went through the congregation and asked for everyone to pitch in toward a heater. I was able to raise the money needed in one night. We put in a few dollars toward it as well. We took the money raised and went and bought a heater.

We let the pastor present the heater to them anonymously as being from the congregation, but they figured out that I had something to do with it. They came up to me after the service and confronted me. They told me, "You did this, didn't you?" I told them that the congregation had pitched in money and that the heater was a gift from the entire congregation. The young lady looked me straight in the eye and said, "I know that you did this." I said that it didn't matter. What was important was the fact that the LORD answered their prayers. They said to me, "It isn't how much money you paid that matters. What is important is that you *listened*." That really stuck with me. It is an important truth.

They took the heater back to Israel with them. They lived in a six-story apartment building. They were on the top floor. The heater was so powerful that they put the heater on the landing outside of their apartment, all of the apartments below them would open their doors, and the heater heated the other apartments. (I think that it was because there was an anointing on it. After all, it had been prayed over.) It was a testimony to everyone that lived there. They trusted the LORD and He blessed them, and He turned them into a blessing to other people.

I challenge you to ask the LORD to help you to really listen to people around you. Sometimes the LORD will give us the opportunity to sow things into other people's lives first so that we can reap it later when we need it. That act of obedience may be the very thing that will open the doors in your life.

THE GAS COMPANY

One day, I came home from work and went to turn on the oven, and it wouldn't work. I looked at the pilot light, and it was out. I tried to light it, and it wouldn't light. I decided to go check the tank to make sure we still had gas. They had just filled the tank up a couple weeks before, but I wanted to be sure. When I looked out the window, I noticed that the gas tank was gone. I couldn't believe it.

I called the gas company. They told me that they took our tank because we had not made a payment in over three months. I told them that was not true, because I had gotten a copy of the cancelled check from my bank that was paid to them twelve days before. I demanded to speak to a manager. They told me that he wasn't available. Well, this went on for weeks. I would call, and they would tell me that the manager wasn't available. The representative told me that I had to pay an additional $350 deposit and another $150 for the gas that had been delivered along with the 18 *percent interest* they were charging me for the unpaid balance. Trust me, 18 percent was an extremely high interest rate, since this was almost twenty years ago.

In the meantime, I was cooking using the microwave, electric skillet, and one electrical burner that we had purchased. It was a challenge, but it was amazing what I could make with those three things.

It turns out that the gas company had started coming by the house every week and was topping off the tank. They then started charging interest on the balance. They told me that they had been doing this all along and that I knew that they were doing this. I told them that I had had an account with them for almost five years and that it had never been done that way. We would call to have the tank filled when it got low. We knew that the tank of gas would last us three to four months. We would take the bill for the tank of gas, divide it into thirds, and pay one third of the bill each month. That way, when we needed gas again, there was no outstanding bill.

Finally, I had had enough. I went to the gas company. They told me that the manager refused to speak to me. They told me that I had better pay the money, and they insisted that they had always done business this way. I asked to see the records to back up what they were saying.

They would not provide any paperwork backing up their claim. They would not budge. The manager would not come out to speak with me. I told them that I was going to wait there for the manager. After an hour of waiting, I started telling the other customers that were there shopping for gas appliances what was happening with the gas company. The manager suddenly appeared to speak with me. He pulled me into an office and told me that I had to give the gas company the money. I asked him to show me the records backing up what they said. He admitted to me that there were no records backing them up. He admitted to me that it had always been done the way that I described. But, he told me, I had to pay the money or else I wasn't going to get the tank back. I told him to keep the tank. He told me, "But you need us, so you have to give us the money."

I told him, "I don't need you. I am a child of God, and you cannot treat a child of God like this." I went on to say, "I can and will live without you and your gas company. Mark my words. This company will see that you cannot treat people this way. This company will see the Hand of God within six months." On my way out, I stomped my feet on the welcome mat to "shake the dirt off of my feet." Within six months, the company was bankrupt and had to close its doors.

The LORD took care of us. A couple of months later, we arrived home, and there was a beautiful new range sitting in our driveway. It was a luxurious model. It had a confectionary stove on top and the oven and stove on the bottom. It was electric. It turns out that a friend of ours, named Steve, who knew our situation, had overheard the owner of the company where he worked talking about the new stove that he had bought his wife. His wife didn't like it, so he was going to give it away to a charity or something. Steve walked up to his boss and explained our situation to him, and the man gave him the stove. We had another friend of ours hook up the electricity, and all of a sudden, we had a better stove than we'd had before. The only place that we could connect it up to was in the hallway, but it was wonderful nonetheless. I was so happy to have a beautiful oven and stove. The LORD had taken care of our needs.

YOU REAP WHAT YOU SOW

The next winter came along, and it had started to get cold in the mobile home. A friend came by from our church. He wanted to give us a really nice sofa that his wife didn't want anymore. When he came in, he mentioned that it was cold in our house. We told him what happened. He started laughing. He said that his wife had told him to get rid of the kerosene heater that had been sitting in their garage, so he had stuck it in the back of his truck. He pulled it off of his truck and gave it to us. So, God took care of us. The first night we used the kerosene heater, we realized what had happened. Ultimately, we sowed a kerosene heater and we reaped a kerosene heater.

Galatians 6:7 says, "Be not deceived; God is not mocked: for whatsoever a man soweth, that shall he also reap." We literally sowed a kerosene heater for the couple that lived in Israel and we reaped a kerosene heater.

"But this I say, He which soweth sparingly shall reap also sparingly; and he which soweth bountifully shall reap also bountifully.... And God is able to make all grace abound toward you; that ye, always having all suf-ficiency in all things, may abound to every good work" (2 Corinthians 9:6, 8).

The LORD promises us here that if we sow bounti-fully that we will have "sufficiency in all things." The word "sufficiency" means to have an adequate supply or to have enough of what we need.

I know many people may say that a kerosene heater is not the way that they would choose to heat their home. I also know many people who say that they would not want to cook in their hallway either. Let me remind you of what the scriptures say. Philippians 4:19 says, "My God shall supply all your *need* according to His riches in glory by Christ Jesus." This scripture clearly doesn't say your *wants*. It says your *need*. God took care of our needs.

CREATIVITY AND WISDOM

Creativity means to produce something through imagination or the ability to bring something new into a situation or place. Whenever I would counsel or pray with someone about parenthood, the one thing that I would pray for was for creativity to parenting.

I know a woman that had serious behavioral problems with her son. One of the biggest problems that she had was that he always wet the bed. He was old enough that he shouldn't have that problem anymore. She prayed and sought the LORD about what to do. He told her to do a couple of different things. One, he told her to start feeding him a lot of cauliflower and broccoli. Sure enough, the boy stopped wetting the bed. The LORD told her to start doing everything with her son. So, he was with her when she was cooking and when she was cleaning. Before long, the other behavior problems stopped. The young man is now a grown man and is very successful. Of course, his wife loves it because he helps with the cooking and the cleaning too.

That story has inspired me. That is why I pray for creativity in parenting. Not all children respond to things the same way. Certainly, not all husbands or wives will respond to things the same way either. That is why we need creativity and wisdom on how to deal with our spouses as well.

Wisdom and creativity go hand in hand. Ecclesiastes 9:16 tells us that wisdom is better than strength. Job 12:16 says that "with Him is strength and wisdom." Proverbs 5:1 says that we should pay attention to His wisdom and listen for His understanding. This means that we need to be seeking His guidance, wisdom, and understanding of things. If we see and understand things how He sees them, we can better know what to do to get through the situation. Job 28 tells us that wisdom and understanding only come from God. There is no wisdom and understanding here on earth that compares to Him. So my prayer for you is that the LORD will show you what to do in each and every difficult situation in your life. Don't try to do anything all on your own. Seek His face.

A LESSON IN HUMILITY

We were going to visit family on vacation. We were going to be gone for two weeks. A friend of ours that lives in Jerusalem was in the United States for a visit. We invited her to stay in our home while we were gone. It worked out great. She would take care of the pets, and then she was close to the other friends and family that she wanted to see without imposing on them. I explained to her that we didn't have a dryer and that the washer had stopped working. She told me that it was okay.

When we returned from our vacation, I saw her taking clothes out of the washer. I asked her, "Oh, did you get the washer fixed?" She said, "No, I just anointed the washer with oil and prayed over it, and it has been working ever since." It was so simple. The LORD finds ways to keep us humble.

"For whosoever exalteth himself shall be abased; and he that humbleth himself shall be exalted" (Luke 14:1).

Matthew 23:12 and Luke 18:14 repeat this same truth. Remember, when God repeats Himself, it means that it is important and that we must pay attention (especially when He repeats himself several times).

"A man's pride shall bring him low: but honour shall uphold the humble in spirit" (Proverbs 29:23).

2 Chronicles 12:12 tells us that when we humble ourselves, God's wrath is turned away from us.

TESTING FOR ENDURANCE

When I went into labor with my last child, I had already experienced enough labor. I had twenty-six hours of labor with my first child, nine hours with my second, and fifty-three hours with my third. Well, I figured that I had learned whatever it was that I was going to learn. *Wrong!*

I had *eighty-four* hours of labor with contractions five minutes apart and closer with my last child. I was really disappointed. The doctors will always tell you that your labors are supposed to get shorter with each subsequent pregnancy. Every woman that I knew had had shorter labors with each delivery. Of course, I also had people in my life who told me this meant I was "in sin." I had other people in my life who told me that I "didn't have enough faith." I got tired of the two sides. I decided to pray about it. I asked the LORD to show me why I had such a long labor. I asked the LORD to show me if I was in sin. I knew that I had faith. I had been "confessing" that I was going to have short labor. I had even been specific. I was confessing and praying daily, "I am going to have this baby quickly and easily, in eight hours of labor or less." I had *eighty-four hours*. Why? The LORD spoke to me the following:

> Count yourself blessed. I am teaching you endurance, my child. Endurance is not a popular lesson in My body. Count yourself blessed that you had a healthy baby at the end.

I would encourage everyone reading this—let the LORD teach you. Rejoice that He loves you and your family, and you will make it. Some of the things that we need to learn in life are not necessarily easy.

Paul says in 2 Timothy 2:10, "Therefore, I endure all things..." He endured so that people would get saved. If we don't ever go through any hardships, how can we witness to the world? The testimony is that we walked through it and that the LORD was there to strengthen us and sustain us. Paul again says in 2 Timothy 4:5 that we must watch all things and "endure afflictions." Once again, it is for the purpose of the ministry.

Hebrews 12:6–7 says, "For whom the LORD loveth He chasteneth, and scourgeth every son whom He receiveth.

If ye endure chastening, God dealeth with you as with sons, for what son is he whom the father chasteneth not?" The word "chastening" means discipline and correction. We know that good earthly parents who love their children must correct and discipline their children, but we don't want God's correction or discipline. We have to endure the correction and the lessons that He wants to teach us. The lessons make us stronger. James says in 5:11, "Behold, we count them happy which endure..." The best fitness trainers in the world will tell you that the best way to become stronger is to do resistance training. We must expect to go through resistance training spiritually as well.

I challenge you to read the "love chapter" (1 Corinthians 13) very carefully. There is a lot more to this chapter than we want to admit. We cannot pick and choose which lessons we need to learn. Bearing things and enduring things are not usually pleasant experiences.

"Beareth all things, believeth all things, hopeth all things, endureth all things" (1 Corinthians 13:7).

> Humble yourselves therefore under the mighty Hand of God, that He may exalt you in due time: Casting all your care upon Him; for He careth for you. Be sober, be vigilant, because your adversary the devil, as a roaring lion, walketh about, seeking whom he may devour: Whom resist steadfast in the faith, knowing that the same afflictions are accomplished in your brethren that are in the world. But the God of all grace, who hath called us

> unto His eternal glory by Christ Jesus, after
> that ye have suffered a while, make you *per-*
> *fect, establish, strengthen, settle you.* To Him be
> glory and dominion forever and ever. Amen.
>
> 1 Peter 5:6–11

This scripture shows us many things. God has to have
dominion (control) over everything in your life. We have
to cast *all* of our cares on Him. We must resist the devil
by being steadfast in our faith. Steadfast means: firm in
our beliefs, firmly fixed, having determination. To be firm,
fixed and determined, you have to be standing for something. We have to stand, knowing that the LORD will get
us through and that everything will be all right. Through
the trials, we are perfected, established, strengthened, and
settled in our faith.

> My son, despise not the chastening of the
> LORD; neither be weary of his correction:
> For whom the LORD loveth He correcteth;
> even as a father, the son in whom he delight-
> eth. Happy is the man that findeth wisdom,
> and the man that getteth understanding. For
> the merchandise of it is better than the mer-
> chandise of silver, and the gain thereof than
> fine gold. She is more precious than rubies:
> and all the things thou canst desire are not to
> be compared unto her.
>
> Proverbs 3:11–15

A HEALING OF THE BRAIN

One of my daughters was a "Houdini" of safety belts. It didn't seem to make any difference how secure we belted her into the high chair or car seat; she would constantly squirm her way free. She fell on her head several times as a toddler, usually from the high chair. We have several family members and friends that would help us try to belt her safely into the high chair, but it wouldn't make any difference. She could get out of the belt very quickly. It didn't ever seem to hurt her.

Well, when she was about seven or so, we noticed that she was having mini seizures. She would be fine, but then she would get this blank look in her eyes, and she couldn't hear you or respond. The seizures would only last a few seconds, and then she would be back to normal. At first, we didn't realize what was happening. When we realized what was going on, the insurance company would not approve for her to go for any testing or treatment for this, and we didn't have any money to pay for the necessary tests. We kept praying for her.

We noticed that the mini seizures became less and less frequent, and eventually, they seemed to stop. When she was twelve years old, she had some bad headaches, and the doctor finally referred her for testing. She had a CT scan, and it showed her brain to be completely normal. Bless the name of the LORD. She was healed. She hasn't had seizures since.

ANTI-FEAR AND ANTI-GRAVITY

Joe worked as a truck driver for a lumber company. The truck they had him drive wasn't always in the best shape. One day, when I was at work, I had this overwhelming feeling of fear. I would hear things like, "Did you tell Joe you loved him this morning?" I rebuked the spirit of fear, but I still had a bad feeling. So, I started praying. I asked God to put Joe and whoever was with him in the palm of His hand.

That was an unusual prayer to pray, since he always did his deliveries alone, but that is what I felt led to pray.

That evening, when I got home from work, I found out what happened. My husband had been out on another delivery in another truck, so his supervisor had loaded the next truck. So he came back with an empty truck and got into the new fully loaded truck and left again. It turned out that the truck was overloaded and not tied down properly. He had to make a delivery in Palm Beach. He was going around a curve very slowly, but the load shifted and the truck ended up rolling. The dangerous part was that the air conditioning in the truck didn't work, so they had the windows down, and the seatbelts were broken. This was back in the day when seatbelts were strongly suggested, not mandatory, and the company Joe worked for only did as little as possible.

There was a man in a car driving down the road from the other direction that saw the truck roll. He pulled over, got out, and ran over to the truck. When he got to the truck and leaned down to look inside (the truck was still upside down), he screamed "What in the world?" My husband responded, "My wife was praying!" You see, my husband and the young man next to him in the truck were still in their seats. Gravity had not even pulled them down. They didn't move from their seats until my husband responded that I had been praying. Then, and only then, did he and the young man with him fall out of their seats, but they weren't hurt. God created gravity, so He can defy it too. They walked away without even a bruise.

By the way, the sheriff that came to the scene of the accident gave the company four citations but no ticket or anything to my husband. That was a blessing. My husband changed jobs after that.

EVERYONE IS SOMEBODY'S CHILD

I was working a three-month-long temporary job at a cancer treatment facility attached to a hospital. We had a patient that would come over from the hospital for radiation treatment for brain cancer. She had a great personality. She was sweet, but you could tell from her rough language that she wasn't a believer. The LORD kept waking me up one night and saying to me that I needed to go pray with her. Finally, I told the LORD that if He wanted me to do that, He would have to arrange for it not to be a conflict of interest with my employer.

I went to work the next day. I was informed that Sue had been moved to the hospice. She had slipped into a coma. I told the LORD that He did great at getting her out of our facility, but He blew it because she was now in a coma. The LORD wouldn't leave me alone. So I went home that night and asked my husband what to do. He told me to go. I got a sitter for the kids (since my husband was going to a prayer meeting) and headed for the hospice.

I got to the hospice around 8:30 p.m. They told me that I had to wait because they had a problem with Sue's IV and were working on it. After a few minutes, one of the directors of the hospice came up to me. She asked me if I was family. I told her no. She asked me how I knew the patient. I told her. She told me that that was amazing. She told me, "People don't come here. Only family comes here, and then they only stay for as little time as possible."

The LORD spoke to me and told me, "This is an indictment of My people. My people should not be scared of death. My people belong here."

After waiting approximately twenty minutes, the nurses came out and told me that I could go in for a short visit. When I walked into the room, I was shocked. I could feel the presence of evil in the room. I had never been exposed to that, since all of my relatives are believers. I had never been around a dying person who wasn't a believer.

I took a hold of her hand. I told her that the LORD had sent me to pray for her. I leaned over and put a dab of anointing oil on her forehead. I prayed this prayer: "LORD, please touch her and take away all of her pain, from the top of her head to the soles of her feet. In Jesus' name. Amen."

When I got done, I found strange words coming out of my mouth. I said to her, "Do you remember hearing about Jesus when you were a child?" I'm thinking to myself, *Why did I ask her a question? She is in a coma. Besides, I don't know anything about her.*

Sue opened her mouth and whispered, "Yes." I almost fainted. In fact, I fell against the wall behind me. It was a good thing that it was only a few inches away. A woman in a coma had just spoken to me.

I then found myself saying to her, "God is up in heaven with outstretched hands, waiting to receive you, but He says that you must first receive His Son. He knows that you cannot pray, so He sent me here to pray with you. If I pray and ask Jesus to come into your heart, will you let Him come in?"

She whispered, "Yes."

I started praying these words: "Lord God, please cleanse Sue's heart from sin. Please cleanse her from the top of her head to the soles of her feet and make her ready to come to heaven. Jesus, please come into her heart and cleanse her from sin. In Jesus' name, Amen."

When I got done, she whispered, "Thank you," and she gently squeezed my hand.

I heard the screech of the demons, and then I saw a pillar of light come into the room through the ceiling. When I looked back down, she appeared to still be in her coma, but she had a look of peace now on her face. I leaned down, gave her a kiss on her cheek, and told her,

"I'll see you when I get to heaven." I went out to my car. I sat in my car and cried for quite a while before I could leave. I do not know all of the reasons for it, but God didn't tell me to pray for her healing. He told me that He wanted her in heaven. She had had a rough life, and she needed to be with Him.

The next morning, I called the hospice to find out how Sue was doing. They connected me to her nurse. The nurse said to me, "She passed away last night."

Before I could stop it, "Hallelujah" popped out of my mouth. I then told the nurse, "I know that sounds strange. I'm sorry." She said she was a Christian and wanted to know what I meant by that. She told me that when she came on her shift late the night before, she could tell a difference in the way Sue looked. They told her that a mysterious redhead had come to visit, stayed only a few minutes, and then left. They told her that after I left, Sue came out of the coma and was resting peacefully and that she no longer needed pain medication. This is incredible, since dying from brain cancer is one of the most painful ways to die. She asked me if I was that redhead, and I said yes. I told her what happened during the visit. She started crying, and she told me that I had no idea what I had done. I said that I did know and that I was really shaken up over the whole thing. I told her that I had come really close to talking myself out of going to the hospice. She told me, "No. You really have no idea what you did." She said that the woman's mother had called from Dayton, Ohio, that morning and was crying on the phone, saying, "Oh no, my daughter died without knowing the Lord."

(I was born in Dayton, Ohio, and raised in a suburb of Dayton.) She told me that she couldn't give me her phone number to call, but that she was going to call Sue's mother back and tell her, "You don't need to weep any longer, your daughter accepted the LORD last night!"

The LORD spoke to me and said these words: "Remember this: everyone is somebody's child, but most importantly, *everyone is my child.* If there is just one praying parent, I will go to the gates of hell and back, but I *will not let your children go.*" It is totally amazing to me that God would take me, who grew up in Dayton, Ohio, to Florida, and I would get the opportunity to pray and lead this woman, who was also from Dayton, Ohio, to the LORD right before she died—in answer to her mother's prayers. I did not know that she was from Dayton, Ohio, beforehand.

We know that we are supposed to be ministering to people. We know that we are supposed to be reaching out to the dying. We are supposed to be snatching people out of the grips of the enemy and introducing them to the LORD. We are not supposed to be scared of death. We know what to do. We need to do it. James 4:17 says, "Therefore to him that knoweth to do good, and doeth it not, to him it is sin."

OUR SON: THE LIVING MIRACLE

When he was four years old, our son, David, was going to preschool. The cancer treatment facility where I worked was only three blocks from the school. My husband would get off of work, pick up Jessica from the babysitter's house, pick up the children from their schools, and then pick me up from work.

So on this day, as usual, my husband went to pick up the children from school. My husband was all excited because the Minnesota Twins were in the World Series, and the second game of the series was on TV that night and also because his parents had just arrived from Minnesota. David's teacher happened to also be from Minnesota. So, she and Joe were busy talking about the World Series, and he heard the side door of the van shut. He thought that David had gotten in the van. He said good-bye to the teacher and got in the van. When he got in the van, he asked the girls, "Everything all set?" and they answered, "Yes." He started to pull away.

It turned out that David had run back to the school building. When he saw Joe pulling away, he ran toward the side of the van and tried to come to a stop next to the van, but he skidded on the wet pavement (it had rained heavily that day) and ended up sliding under the van. Joe couldn't see any of this because of the blind spots on the sides of the van.

The chrome on the bottom of the van put a nasty groove into his face, and the back wheel of the van ran over his chest. When Joe felt the van run over something, he immediately stopped, jumped out, and ran around the van. There was David, blood spurting from his mouth and his eyes rolled back. The teacher panicked and picked David up off the pavement and ran for the office. Another teacher had called 911, so an ambulance arrived in a few minutes.

David had no vital signs. They put David on a stretcher and put him in the ambulance, and the teacher jumped into the ambulance with him. The paramedics thought she was his mother and didn't question her. Joe ran to pick me up from work, and we took off for the hospital where

David was being taken. It was horrible. Of course, our family immediately started praying. The paramedics estimate that David was without any vitals for eight minutes. They had pretty much given up all hope of him coming back and being normal.

David's teacher admitted to us later that when she got into the ambulance, she was an atheist. She had been an atheist her entire adult life. When she saw the paramedics trying to revive him in the ambulance, she said to herself, *This boy talks about Jesus too much. If Jesus is real, He won't let David die.* In a split second, all vitals started and were normal. David's teacher got out of the ambulance a believer. She said that when she saw David instantly healed and restored, she had no choice but to believe.

When we got to the hospital, it was really terrible seeing that my son's clothes had been cut off of him and that there were tubes attached to him everywhere. They ran every test on him twice, because they couldn't find anything wrong with him. (Joe was out in the waiting area with our other three children and his parents.)

The doctors and nurses kept asking me, "Did anyone see the accident?" I kept telling them, repeatedly, that there were at least thirty people at the school who witnessed it. Finally, I asked a doctor why everyone kept asking me that. He told me that it was because they couldn't find anything wrong with David (except for the cut into his face). I told him that was because Jesus had healed him. The doctor told me that he believed me. I was in a large ER area divided by curtains in the largest hospital in the county, so there were a lot of people who heard me. I was surprised to hear "Praise the LORD," "Hallelujah," and "Thank you LORD" from people in the ER behind the other curtains. After David was given the all clear, Joe took our other children home.

I knew we truly had a miracle when the paramedics came back a few hours later. When they saw David sitting up and drinking ice water, they started crying. They told me that it was moments like that that made their job rewarding. That is when they told me the whole story about how bad off things had been.

Well, the hospital then transferred my son upstairs to the "step down" unit. They said that he was too well to be in the Intensive Care Unit, but since he had been run over by a van, they couldn't put him in a regular room. The hospital then told me that since they were doing renovations to that part of the hospital, they didn't have room for me to stay with my son. I was extremely upset. My four-year-old son had been through this horrific accident, and they would not let me stay in the hospital with him. Hospital security took me out of the hospital. They put me in a taxi, and the hospital paid for the taxi to take me home.

When I got home, I realized immediately why God sent me there. Joe was in shambles. He felt so terrible. I put my arms around him and told him repeatedly that it was just an unfortunate accident. He cried out to the

LORD, "LORD, people lose children all the time. Why did you give us our son back?"

God spoke to us and said, "You reap what you sow. You gave me my daughter [Sue] back in the hospice. I gave you David back. Everyone is somebody's child, and *everyone is my child.* You reap what you sow."

"Be not deceived; God is not mocked for whatsoever a man soweth, that shall he also reap" (Galatians 6:7).

Joe then cried out to the LORD and said, "But, God, how can I face my son again after what happened?"

God spoke to us and said, "What you did to your son was an accident, but what I did to My Son was on purpose. That is why when Jesus was hanging on the cross and the heavens had been opened, Jesus could see Me on My throne, that I had turned My back to Him because I could not bear to watch Him die. When He saw me turn away, that is when He said, 'My God, My God, why have You forsaken Me?'" Meditate on that for a while.

By the way, there was a groove across my son's face that went from his upper lip up at an angle to his right temple. The doctor gave me a cream and told me that it would help "minimize scarring," but that he would probably end up needing plastic surgery. God healed David of that too. He only has a small scar right under his nose, about one millimeter wide, that he can see if he gets right up to the mirror and looks for it. It is his reminder that God healed him and gave him his life back.

Throughout the Bible, God teaches a principle of stopping and remembering. All of the feasts and holidays that the Jewish people celebrate involve stopping and taking time to remember what God has done and taking time to say thank you. It is really important to do this. I challenge you to do a Bible study surrounding the principal of saying thank you to God for what He has done. Because our family has studied the Old Testament extensively, we understand this principle. Every year during the World Series (since that is when his accident took place), we stop as a family. We talk about the memories that we have about what happened in our family, and we all stop to give praise to the LORD for giving us our son back. David also talks to each of his sisters about the event, and it is a great time of appreciation for the LORD's goodness and to reflect on His miracle-working power.

I encourage you to do the same thing. Is there an important event that took place in your family? I challenge you to take time each year to stop and give special thanks to the LORD for what He has done. Don't worry or fret about the *exact* moment. Sometimes we can't even remember the exact day. It doesn't matter. Get as close as you can to the day, and God will be absolutely thrilled that you take the time to remember Him and His goodness. In our situation, we take time during the World Series. We talk to our friends and other family members and remind them about the miracle that happened. It doesn't matter if it is the exact day. *Just take time to remember God's greatness.*

"Bless the LORD, O my soul: and all that is within me, bless His holy Name. Bless the LORD, O my soul, and *forget not all His benefits*" (Psalms 103:1–2).

Here are two examples from the scriptures of doing this. There are many more. When God has something repeated in the scriptures, it is for a reason. When it is repeated several times, it is important, and God wants us to pay attention. God definitely wants us to take time to thank Him. We should take time to thank Him regularly for specific events in our life and we need to be thankful every day for everything that He has given us. The scriptures tell us that we are to tell people about what the LORD has done. That is one of the main reasons that I wrote this book. I am broadcasting all of the great things that the LORD has done for our family.

> Give thanks unto the LORD, call upon His name, make *known His deeds among the people.* Sing to Him, sing psalms unto Him, *talk ye of all His wondrous works.* Glory ye in His holy name: let the heart of them rejoice that seek the LORD. Seek the LORD and His strength, seek His face continually. *Remember His marvelous works that He has done, his wonders,* and the judgments of His mouth.... O give thanks to the LORD; for He is good, for His mercy endureth forever.
>
> 1 Chronicles 16:8–12, 34 (emphasis mine)

> O give thanks to the LORD; call upon His name: *make known His deeds among the people.* Sing unto Him, sing psalms unto Him: *talk ye of all His wondrous works.* Glory ye in His holy name: let the heart of them rejoice that seek the LORD. Seek the LORD and His

strength: seek His face evermore. *Remember His marvelous works that He hath done; his wonders,* and the judgments of His mouth.

Psalm 105:1–5 (emphasis mine)

Once again, He repeats Himself. Whenever something is repeated in the Word, it means that it is important.

THE RIPPLE EFFECT

I got a call one day. A friend of mine asked me if I remembered meeting Elizabeth at her house. We had gone there for dinner, and our friend had introduced Elizabeth to us there. She was an angry person. She did a lot of yelling, especially at the children. I told my friend that I remembered the lady. She told me that Elizabeth was in the intensive care unit at the hospital. I told her that I would go to see her.

The doctors had said that there was nothing more they could do for her. She had had heart problems for many years, and they knew she wouldn't survive any heart surgeries anyway due to her age (she was in her eighties) and her other health problems.

I prayed for Elizabeth that night, and the LORD spoke to me. He told me *not* to say anything about Jesus to her. I worked in a building next to the hospital she was in. On my lunch hour the next day, I ate my lunch as quickly as possible, put on my white lab jacket, and ran over to the hospital. I went upstairs and walked right into the Intensive Care Unit and right into her room. No one stopped me because I looked and acted like I belonged there.

When I got in the room, I said hi to her and asked her if she remembered me. She said, "Yes, and I don't want to hear any of that Jesus stuff."

I replied to her, "I know. That's not what I'm here for."

She then asked me, "Then why are you here?"

I said, "Because I love you."

She replied, "Well then, sit down."

I sat down with her, and we talked about the weather, my children, her children, her grandchildren, and whatever she wanted to talk about. On the third day I was there with her, a nurse came into the room and asked her who I was. She told the nurse, "It's a religion thing. Leave us alone." The nurse winked at me and left. No one ever said another word to me about being there, and I knew then that something was getting through to her. I went and spent my lunch hour with her Monday through Friday that week. I also spent my lunch hour with her each day of Monday through Thursday of the next week. The doctor then said that he was sending her home on

Friday morning "to die," because she had decided that she didn't want to die in the hospital.

On Thursday evening, the friend that had called me and asked me to visit Elizabeth went to the hospital to see her. She says that as soon as she walked into the room, Elizabeth said, "I'm ready to accept Jesus now." She prayed and accepted the LORD that night. It was so exciting.

The only strange thing was what happened next. My friend called me to tell me what happened. I was so excited. I was crying, laughing, and shouting Hallelujah all at the same time. Then my friend told me, "I don't know what you are so excited about." I said that I was thrilled that all of our efforts had paid off. She then said, "You had nothing to do with this. It was me and my husband that are responsible for this." I was stunned. I was totally caught off guard. It was one of the strangest things I have ever heard. I told her that it didn't matter who got credit for this lady's salvation. What was important was that she received the LORD and that she was going to heaven. My experience is that when people accept the LORD, there has usually been a "team" of God's people involved. But ultimately, it is Jesus that saves. All glory needs to go to Him, our Savior and Redeemer.

"And whatsoever you do in word or deed, do all in the name of the LORD Jesus, giving to God and the Father by Him" (Colossians 3:17).

The incredible thing was that when the woman went home (she lived with one of her daughters), her daughter freaked out. She called the rest of her siblings up (that lived in New York) and told them, "You have to come home quick. Mom is dying, but something more serious than that is going on. *She is nice now!* I don't know what to think." Her family arrived, and they sat down with Mom and had a long talk with her. They all got saved, one by one. All of her children and grandchildren got saved. All it takes is one transformation in a family to make a difference.

SHOPPING MIRACLES

I firmly believe that every believer ought to pray before they go shopping. It doesn't matter what kind of shopping. When we pray and ask the LORD to help us, He will guide us as to what to buy and how to make our money stretch. I believe a lot more money would be available for giving away if we were careful. Also, we would be able to get out of debt quicker. I think that many believers don't pray before they shop just because they don't want to hear what God might say. I believe in the necessity to pray for creativity. It is amazing what can happen when we pray for creativity. I am going to give you a few examples of what I mean.

We had been attending a World Conference in Florida, and we had gotten to know this wonderful couple from Scotland. I really felt that the LORD had laid it on my heart to do something for them. We had very little money at the time, so I didn't know what to do. I prayed about it. Then I went to the mall to look around for something.

This gentleman approached me and asked me if I would do a survey on these new plastic containers that were coming out. I told him that I wouldn't mind. I had to test and evaluate three plastic containers (like ease of taking the lids off, ease of putting the lids back on, how easy it was to pour cereal out of the containers, etc.). At the end of the testing, they gave me a gift certificate to a department store in the mall. I went down to that store and found this really expensive, beautiful set of gold towels that were marked way down. They were the last ones like them in the store. I had a coupon that I had gotten out of the paper for free gift wrapping at the same store. So, I bought the towels with the gift certificate and used the gift-wrapping coupon and had it wrapped. It was beautiful.

That night, I asked the lady to come out to my car after the service. I pulled out the gift, and she was shocked. She knew that we had been praying for the LORD to help us financially, so she certainly didn't expect anything from me. When she opened the box, she got so excited. She asked me, "How did you know that one of my bathrooms is decorated in gold?" I told her that I didn't know! She asked me, "How in the world did you ever afford these beautiful towels?" I told her not to worry, because God had supplied them. I calculated how much the towels had been marked down. They were marked down 95 *percent.*

When the LORD lays someone on your heart and asks you to do something for them, please don't ignore Him. Just pray and ask the LORD to show you what to do. If you don't have money, it doesn't matter. God will supply the seed for you to sow! Just make sure that when He does supply the seed, you don't devour it. I could have used the gift certificate for something for our family, but that isn't what God wanted. He wouldn't have blessed that. So, it doesn't matter if something costs money or not. It just matters that you are giving of yourself.

A few years ago, I volunteered to feed the cast and crew of the Christmas play at the church that we were attending at that time. There were restaurants that were providing food for the other nights, but there was one night left that needed to be taken care of. It wasn't an ordinary Christmas play. It was done very professionally. There were 115 members of the cast and crew, plus a few extra family members that are at the church during the dress rehearsals. I knew immediately that the LORD wanted me to do it. I thoroughly enjoy doing things like that. I have provided dinner for several large groups of people over the years. Most of the time, I have to feed the people by a specific meal plan, but this time the church said that I could feed them whatever I wanted to.

The LORD immediately started supplying amazing things. The first thing that the LORD supplied for free (with coupons, of course) was five boxes of a deluxe frozen vegetable mix that had broccoli, cauliflower, carrots, butter, and garlic in it. He supplied me more boxes of the vegetables later on to add to that. My daughter called me a couple of days before Thanksgiving and told me that a grocery store up where she lives was having a deal where you got $10 off your turkey when you bought two twenty-four packs of soda. I told her that I already had the turkey taken care of for Thanksgiving.

We went to my daughter's house to spend the weekend after Thanksgiving with her and her family. I went to the store, and they still had the special going, so I picked up a turkey that was 12.8 pounds. It was supposed to cost approximately eleven dollars, so I thought that it was a pretty good deal. After the dinner at the church was over, I went back over my receipts and realized that God had done something truly amazing. The turkey rang up for $5.12, and I got ten dollars off. So basically, I got paid $4.88 to take a 12.8-pound turkey home to feed God's people. To me, that is fun.

I went to the bread store a couple of days before the dinner, and I was praying that the LORD would show me what to get. The manager of the store told me that she had too many of the twenty-four packs of rolls. She said that she was selling them for sixty-nine cents. That is pretty reasonable, so I bought eight packs of them. I knew then that I would be feeding them some kind of turkey sandwich. I then went to another grocery store that had tortillas on sale and got several large packs of them. The LORD continued guiding me and helping me. I let Him form my menu.

My sister called me and said that she had gone home and opened her recipe file to make some cookies, and the recipe file flipped open to a recipe that she had forgotten she had for homemade turkey barbecue sandwiches.

The cost of the entire dinner, including seasonings, butter, milk, etc., was $34.90. It was incredible. I ended up with six eight-foot tables full of food. I did have a small amount of leftovers, but not much. I only tell you this story so that you can believe for miracles in your shopping too.

I do want to mention that my sister, Linda, made home-made cookies, because she is a helpful, considerate person. The cookies are not included in the cost of the dinner, since she brought them with her when she came to help me serve the dinner. Also, the church supplied the drinks.

Another example of the LORD blessing us through unusual situations is when my husband had to have outpatient surgery done on his left knee the week before Christmas. When he was sent home from the hospital, they gave me a prescription for prescription-strength pain reliever. I took the prescription, along with a coupon good for a gift card, to a local pharmacy. The coupon was for a twenty-five-dollar gift card with a new prescription. I turned in the prescription, paid the ten-dollar co-pay, and was given a twenty-five-dollar gift card.

I took the gift card home, went through the ad, and matched coupons out of my coupon file to it. I found some wonderful things that also gave you "extra bucks" when you bought them. So, I went through and spent the twenty-five-dollar gift card (using coupons); then I went through and got more things with the extra bucks (using coupons). In total, I paid the ten-dollar co-pay for Joe's medication, and I got seventy-two dollars' worth of items for free. Of course, that meant that all four of my adult children got large packs of batteries and other things that may not be the typical Christmas gifts, but they certainly are the useful kind. In fact, almost half of the one large pack of batteries was used by the end of Christmas day. They were already in my grandchildren's toys.

> Rejoice in the LORD always: and again I say, Rejoice. *Let your moderation be known unto all men.* The LORD is at hand. Be careful for nothing; but in every thing by prayer and supplication with thanksgiving let your requests be made known unto God. And the peace of God, which passeth all understanding, shall keep your hearts and minds through Christ Jesus.
>
> Philippians 4:4–7

Moderation is a word that not too many people know about anymore. The word *moderation* actually means *to lessen the extremeness or intensity or to be less severe.* We can't do this if we are spending everything we have on ourselves.

Isaiah 58 tells us that we need to take care of the poor and hungry. We are to clothe the naked. If we do this, we are promised the blessings. How can we do this if we are not careful with our money? If you have a lot of money but you waste a large portion of it and use a tiny amount of it to help the needy, you are still guilty. We are expected to be careful with our money and to pray for the LORD to help us to further the kingdom of God. The blessings that are guaranteed in Isaiah 58 are for the people who do this.

This is a list of the blessings that are listed in Isaiah 58:

1. Great health

2. Righteousess

3. Glory of the LORD

4. LORD hears you and answers you

5. Darkness will vanish

6. LORD's guidance

7. Provision in times of drought

8. Satisfy our souls

9. Never run out of provision

10. Blessed family lines

This list is incredible. Are you wasting what God has given you? Are you being selfish with what He has given you?

In Florida, I knew of a very rich man. You didn't know it by the way he dressed or by what car he drove, or even by the house that he lived in. I only knew because I had found out information about his business. He was giving away tens of thousands of dollars to needy families in the church. He had three children and he lived in a four bed-room, two bath house. He had two nice used cars. He had a moderately sized camper that they used for vacations. All of these things are nice, but not extravagant. I could see that the LORD's blessings were in his life because he used what the LORD gave him to bless others.

One day, a man that I knew from church approached me as I was leaving work. He was going into the business as I was going out. He told me that he had heard that I get a lot of answers to prayer. He asked me if I would agree in prayer with him. I asked him what he wanted prayer for. He said that he wanted a seven bedroom house, a new BMW, a new Mercedes Benz and a new van. He said that he wanted to buy all name brand clothes for his three chil-dren. I asked him why he wanted all of that and he said that it was because it would mean that he was successful and he could feel good about himself. I told him that I could not agree in prayer with him for all of that.

The purpose of buying a house, cars and nice clothes is *not* for the purpose of looking and feeling successful. It certainly isn't so that we can feel good about ourselves. We are not supposed to base how we feel about ourselves on what we have. I challenge you to ask the LORD to show you the motives hidden in your heart. You may have good intentions, but will you follow through on the good intentions.

I met a millionaire, but I didn't know that he was one at the time. My parents knew him and they knew that he was a millionaire. He always wore the same two piece suit. He always looked nice, but never fancy. *My parents told me that he made his money to fund the work of the* LORD, *not for personal gain.* What an example for us to follow.

I was visiting a church in another city where my daughter went to church. A friend of hers asked me if I could agree in prayer with him. I asked him what he needed. He said that he wanted the LORD to prosper him tremendously. I asked him why. He said that he was starting a ministry to homeless people in that city and he wanted to have the money to support his outreach. I immediately grabbed his hands and started praying. He did prosper. He did start that ministry and he continues to do the work of the LORD in that city and he provides almost all of the money needed to sustain the ministry. Isaiah 58 tells us that we need to take care of the poor and hungry and clothe the naked.

In the movie *Schindler's List*, Oskar Schindler says something at the end of the movie that is very moving. He had sold almost everything that he had in order to buy Jewish people to save from the Holocaust. He grabs the gold pin on his lapel and he says that he doesn't know why he didn't sell the pin. After all, it would have bought and saved another Jew. He turns to his car and asks the same question as to why did he not sell the car and buy more Jews.

How can we do the work of the LORD if we are not careful with our money? Ask the LORD to show you where the excess is in your life. If you have a lot of money but you waste a large portion of it and only use a tiny amount of it to help the needy, you are still guilty. We are expected to be careful with our money and to pray for the LORD to help us to further the kingdom of God.

We need to remember that we are supposed to live our life with the world in mind. By that I mean that we need to remember that we are supposed to be using what the LORD gives us not just for our personal needs but for the needs of the people of this world.

I challenge you—don't just believe God for miracles in your health. Believe God for creativity in your shopping. All of the money belongs to Him anyway. He wants more of the money doing things in the kingdom of God.

"He that giveth unto the poor shall not lack: but he that hideth his eyes shall have many a curse." Proverbs 28:27

THE GERMAN CONNECTION

The LORD had spoken to me the same night that He had spoken to Joe back in college. God spoke to both of us and told us that He was raising up people with German heritage to bless Israel so that He could spare Germany from destruction. Joe and I happen to both be half German. You see, God is a just God. If we were back in the Old Testament times, Germany would be an archaeological find by now because of the Holocaust. So, in order for Him to spare Germany, He has to have what I call an "avenue of mercy." When people of German heritage bless Israel, mercy can be given to Germany.

We had this word from the LORD back in 1980. Since then, we have met people from all over the world who were told the same thing—the same year—people all the way from Canada to Guatemala. Once, a couple came up to us at a conference and told us that the LORD had told them to ask us why they were called by God to bless Israel and the Jewish people in Jamaica. I immediately said to them, "Oh, you must be German." They were astonished. They said "Yes. We are of German heritage. How did you know that?" So I explained to them what was going on.

When we went to Israel, we met two young people who were there from Germany. It turns out that God had spoken to two wealthy German businessmen back in 1980 and told them to rise up and bless Israel in order to spare Germany from being destroyed. They were close friends, so they put their finances together and set up a program where they finance volunteers going to Israel and living there for a year at a time. The two German businessmen pay all of the volunteers' expenses while in Israel. The volunteers then work with the Israeli government, and one of the things they do is deliver meals to the elderly. The LORD has spoken to people all over the world about blessing Israel. Israel is obviously very important to Him.

ISRAEL'S BLESSINGS

The LORD spoke to us at the beginning of 1992 and told Joe and me that we would be going to Israel in July for three weeks (without the children). We started looking for inexpensive flights, but there weren't any. We had had a really rough year financially, and we didn't have any money, but we were still looking. We called all of the airlines that flew to Israel, and we had found nothing reasonable. It kept getting closer and closer to July. Joe had told his employer that he would be going, but he didn't know exactly when yet. He had two weeks paid vacation, but the third week wouldn't be paid.

When the beginning of July came around, we still didn't know when we were going. I worked for a Jewish doctor at that time who had a policy that anyone taking more than one week off at a time would be automatically fired. Also, he expected you to take your vacations around his vacation schedule. I knew that I would most likely be fired for going to Israel. For that reason, I had not yet told my employer about the trip.

I had a cousin at that time who was a travel agent. We contacted him, and he started looking for a flight for us. The cheapest flight he could find was $1,200 per person. We knew that was too much money. It finally came to the point that we had to tell our employers an approximate day that we were leaving, because it was the second week of July. We still didn't have any reservations or any money. It was terrifying telling people when they all thought that we were crazy.

One night, I went back into work after dinner to do extra work, and the doctor was still there. I knew I had to tell him. So I told him I was going on vacation at the end of July. He had been scheduled to take a week-long vacation at that time, so he initially responded by saying that he had cancelled his vacation. I told him that I wasn't canceling mine. He said that he understood that, so he would try to live without me for the week. I told him that it wasn't for one week; it was for three weeks. He turned beet red and yelled at me that it would mean I was fired. I told him that was okay. I told him, "Israel was, is, and always shall be more important than you or anything else on this earth." He took off running from the front reception area back down the hall to his office. My office was down the same hall and was off of his office, so I followed him.

After a couple of minutes, I said to him, "You know what else, Doctor?"

He said, "No, what?"

I said to him, "*And*—I'm not Jewish!" At that, he started shaking really badly and dropped everything he was carrying. He got down on his knees and was trying to gather his papers and things. I could hear him talking to himself. He was saying things like, "I know she's Jewish. She had a Passover seder. She celebrated Yom Kippur."

Finally he asked me, "*Then why are you the way you are?*"

I told him, "Because God told me to be." He got really quiet. In the meantime, I had sat down at my desk and was getting ready to do more transcription. After a couple of minutes, he asked me if I had anyone to cover my work while I was gone. I told him that I did have someone lined up, and I told him the name. He told me that he knew the lady and that that would be fine.

He asked me, "How in the world are you able to afford paying for six people to go to Israel?" I told him that it was just my husband and I going. He asked me what was happening with our four children. I told him that two friends were each taking two children. He asked me how I could afford the childcare. I told him that my friends were doing it for free. He was shocked. He yelled at me, "How are you getting people to care for your children for free when I can't even get people to watch my children and get paid for it?" I told him that my husband and I had sacrificed for people all of our married life and that I wasn't going to apologize in any way for taking this trip.

He then asked me how we could afford for my husband and I to go to Israel for three weeks. At the time, we still didn't have any money for the trip. But, I found myself telling him, "Our friends are paying our way." The doctor said he would hold my job for me.

The next day, the head nurse came into my office and asked me when my husband and I would be going to Israel. I told her that I just knew that it would be before the end of the month. She was shocked. She didn't understand why I would tell my boss I was going when I didn't have reservations. She asked me why. I explained to her that we didn't have the money yet but that we would have the money and the reservations when God decided that we needed them. So every day she would come into my office and ask me, "Do you have the money yet?" and I would say no. She would then say, "Then you are not going!" She would then walk out. It was really scary.

Finally, it came up to the next to last Saturday of the month. I was at work doing extra work so that I would have as much work done as possible before my trip. My husband was at home in the rocking chair. Joe heard the LORD speak to him audibly. He said, "I always wanted you to fly El Al." (That is Israel's official airline.) Joe said, "We have tried El Al!"

God spoke to him again and said, "Call El Al now!" Joe was thinking that this was crazy, since my cousin, Rob, had just spoken with a representative from El Al the day before and was told that it was $1,200 per person.

Joe picked up the phone and called El Al. He first asked if they had any flights left the next week for flying from Miami to Tel Aviv. The lady said that they did have one flight open and that was on Sunday evening (eight days away), which was great. Joe then asked how much the flight was, and the reservation clerk said, "Six hundred dollars per person." Joe was shocked. He asked again, and she said that it was $600 per person. Joe told her to book the reservation. She asked him how he was going to pay, and he said that he didn't have the money yet. She said that she was going to do something nice for us and put a hold on the reservations, but it would have to be paid by Friday (two days before we would be flying out).

Joe called my cousin, Rob, and told him that we had reservations. Rob was shocked, so he called El Al. They told him that we did have reservations and that the price for the tickets had been dropped to $600 per person for only four hours, just to fill up that one particular flight. So he called Joe back and told him.

Later that night, one of our Jewish friends, whom we hadn't seen in over a year, came knocking on our door. We were so surprised to see him. He said that he had heard we were going to Israel and wanted to know if it was too late to help us with our trip. We said no. He gave us $150. That was the beginning of the miracle.

Rob decided to step out in faith with us. He printed the tickets on Monday, overnighted them to me at the doctor's office, and I sent out a postdated check dated for Friday, since Rob needed the money by then. On Tuesday, the head nurse came into my office and said that an overnight envelope had just arrived for me. I went out to the reception area, ripped open the envelope, and pulled out our tickets. Everyone in the office was there. I waved them around and was laughing. The nurse said to me, "I thought you didn't have the money?" I said, *"I don't, but I have the tickets!"* It was a truly exciting moment for me.

Money was coming in every day. I ran into people at the grocery store that gave me money. We had friends show up at our home with money. The last bit of money came in for the tickets on Friday morning, and I deposited it into our account. Rob cashed the check in Minnesota on Friday afternoon, and we flew out on Sunday evening. We still didn't have much money left, but we knew that God had not taken us that far to let us down.

On Friday, the head nurse came into my office and said, "We discussed you at the meeting today. We decided that none of us have ever met someone like you before. You are a woman of God." I was shocked. I didn't feel like a "woman of God." I had been nervous, and many times, I had felt so weak that I felt like I was going to faint.

I had laid down my reputation, thinking that everyone would think that I was crazy. There were a few other "crazy" people who were willing to stand by us and support us, but not many. The last couple of weeks were nerve wracking. We had people that were praying with us every day. Believe me, there weren't very many people willing to stand with us. Be willing to lay down your reputation to obey God. It is amazing what will happen.

We had been in contact with our friends in Israel. We had housing lined up for two weeks, but we didn't know where we would be going for the last week.

We would be spending the first two days in a suburb of Tel Aviv, staying with friends while we recovered from the time change. We would then be in Jerusalem, house sitting for friends of ours who were going out of the country on a ministerial trip for eight days. We would then be staying with other friends in Jerusalem for two days. We were then going to Tiberias. We would be staying in an apartment there for three days. The apartment there was already reserved by someone else for the following week. The apartment is reserved on a first-come, first-served basis, and the other people had called and reserved it before we had. We didn't know where we would end up.

We had gotten a "shopping list" from all of our friends in Israel. There were certain things they couldn't get there that they wanted. They were willing to reimburse us for the expense, but we were not going to take their money.

On Sunday morning, we dropped off the children at the two homes where they were staying. We lived in a mobile home at the time, and it was hurricane season, so we had put together a box of our most important papers and were dropping them off at a friend's house that was "hurricane reinforced" for safekeeping. My friend's boyfriend was there, and he asked me what our schedule was for the day. I explained to him that we had a shopping list of things that our friends in Israel needed, so we were going to go shopping. We would then go home and pack up the car. We would then be going to Ft. Lauderdale, and our friends there were taking us to the airport. As we were pulling out of the driveway, he ran out to stop us. He pulled out his wallet and said that he wanted to bless people in Israel by paying for the things they needed. He pulled out all of the money he had and gave it to us. We then went shopping, but we purposely didn't keep track of how much we were spending. We then went to Ft. Lauderdale, and our friends there took us out to dinner and then took us to the Miami airport. Their car was in the repair shop for major repairs, so they were going to use our car until we returned.

While we were on the plane, I did pull out the receipts and add them up. We ended up with thirty-four cents left from what the man had given us. We flew to Israel with $150 total in money.

The second day in Israel is when we went to a Bible study with our friends, and that is where we met the two young Germans that I mentioned earlier. We were having a great trip. We were very careful with our money. We walked virtually everywhere. The only time we got on buses was when we were going from one town to another.

We found out on our second day in Tiberias that the people who were supposed to be staying in the apartment after us had cancelled. This meant we had the apartment for another week, but we were running out of money.

We had set aside enough money to get us back to the airport but that is all the money we had left. So, we figured that we were done sightseeing and would be fasting for the next week. The phone rang in the apartment, and the lady on the phone asked me if I was Debbie Braga. I told her yes, and she told me that she had gotten a call from a mutual friend of ours in Jerusalem named Julie. Julie had asked her and her husband to call us. She asked me if they could come pick us up the next day and take us to the Saturday morning service at their congregation and then have us over for lunch. I said that we would be happy to go. I was thinking, *Yes, another meal! Hallelujah!*

After the service, we went to their house for lunch. When we arrived, a friend of theirs from Germany, who had just arrived from the airport, came in to have lunch with us. We had a great time of fellowship with everyone. At the end of the lunch, the German lady went upstairs and came back down with an envelope in her hand. She handed me the envelope. She said that a friend of hers had handed her that envelope at the airport in Germany. Her friend had instructed her to pray about whom to give it to in Israel. She told her that she knew there was someone in Israel who was supposed to have the envelope. This lady said that the LORD spoke to her and told her that it was for us. It had writing on the outside of the envelope. She said that it said, "To be a blessing" in German. She told us not to open it until we were back in the apartment. We opened it later, back in the apartment, and it had 500 German marks in it. We didn't know how much money that was. The next day, we took it to the bank and had it exchanged into shekels, so we had plenty of money for the remaining time in Israel. But we were still careful with the money.

We went to Israel with $150 and came back after spending three weeks there with $350. Only God can do that. I believe that it is a miracle.

But we came back to a lot of bills. Our miracle wasn't over yet. There were a couple of surprises that God had prepared for us when we returned.

First of all, when I came home and checked my bank statement, I was surprised to find that $300 had appeared in our bank account. This had happened before. I took my bank statement to the bank and explained to the bank manager that we had been out of the country, so it had to be a mistake. We certainly weren't anywhere near a bank to make a deposit. Our paychecks were not direct deposited, besides the fact that they would not be an exact amount like that. The bank manager once again told me that I must have made a mistake. So I waited a month, and the money was still there. The bank manager once again added the money to my checkbook and told me to count the money as ours.

One of the bills we had was a huge phone bill. It had cost a lot of money to call Israel and arrange our trip with our friends. So I called the phone company to make payment arrangements for the phone bill. I was put on hold for a long time.

In the meantime, I had looked at the phone bill and had noticed some new charges on there. When the man came on the line, he asked me why I was calling. I told him that I wanted to make payment arrangements. I told him that I was also curious as to why there were charges on my phone bill for three-way calling and call waiting. He said, "Ma'am, I hope you are a Christian, because I could get fired for what I am getting ready to say." I told him that I was a Christian and that, in fact, we had just gotten back from Israel. He said, "Ma'am, you don't want to pay this bill. This could be God's answer to your financial needs!" He said that he would put our account "into review" and that in the meantime, we wouldn't have to pay anything on the bill. He said that while we were in Israel, the state of Florida had come down on the phone company about putting unwanted charges on people's phone bills. I told him that was great. He told me to expect a call in six to eight weeks. I was thrilled.

I didn't hear from the phone company for three months. In the meantime, we didn't have to pay anything on our phone bills.

Hurricane Andrew had hit in Miami, fifty three miles from where we lived, and so there were a lot of things that were delayed at that time. I certainly wasn't worried about paying the phone company. Finally, they called me. The lady told me that she was sorry for the inconvenience but that they were sending me a check for $1,353. I asked her why. She told me that the state of Florida ordered them to pay back all of the unwanted charges on people's phones with interest. I asked them how long they thought the unwanted charges had been on the phone. They named a month and year that I knew was incorrect. They said the unwanted charges had been there for over three years. The time that they said the unwanted charges were put on our phone was at a time when I was working part time and my husband had just lost his job. I informed the phone company representative that I knew that that was incorrect, since my husband had been unemployed and I had checked the phone company records particularly carefully due to that fact. She said that she appreciated my honesty but that they had to go by what the phone company computer told them.

I asked them what was going to happen with July, August, September, October, and November's bills. She told me that the phone company was paying all of those "due to all of the inconvenience" that they had put us through. It was another miracle. We made more money off of the phone company than we could have made from interest on a savings account from a bank.

OBEDIENCE BRINGS BLESSINGS

We had moved into a two-bedroom mobile home when we had only one child. We had three more children while living there. It was cramped, to say the least. We had been praying for a financial miracle to take place. God wasn't done yet. Eight months after we got back from Israel, my mother-in-law inherited $33,500 and gave us $32,000. With that money, we moved out of the mobile home, paid off all of our debts, and paid for two nice, used cars.

It was incredible. It is amazing what God will do for you when you obey him. Be willing to lay everything down and trust Him.

I will warn you though. We lost almost all of our "friends." Many of our friends had started telling us that we were crazy when we started planning our trip to Israel with no money, and they continued telling us we were crazy when they said that we should save our money and apply ourselves to getting out of the mobile home. We soon realized how few true friends we had. So, be prepared. When you decide to live by faith and do something that God is leading you to do, you will get hassled from people in the "church." In fact, you may get more trouble from people in the church than you get from people in the "world." It was people in the "world," for the most part, who would tell us how much they admired what we were doing. We had a select few in the church who stood by us.

God told us that He was taking us through an experience similar to what Jesus went through. He ministered to the multitudes and traveled with the disciples, but he was truly close to only a *few* select individuals. He also had many of the people close to Him try to talk Him out of doing what He had come to Earth to do. He also had the one person ultimately betray Him.

Ephesians 6:6–8 tells us that we must do the will of God from our heart and that we must do service to the Lord and *not* to men. We only need to fear God, *not* men. Hebrews 13:6 says, "… The Lord is My Helper, and I will not fear what man shall do unto me."

The safest place to be in the world is the place that the LORD tells you to be. The problem is that we assume things. I heard an excellent sermon once about this problem. The man was a minister in a very dangerous country. He said that at one point there had been a lot of killing going on in his country. There were mines being laid in the fields and streets. The invading army was looking to kill the Christians in the area. He said that a lot of people in his congregation got scared and fled. Other people prayed about it and decided to stay. All of the people that fled lost everything. Some of them died. Out of all the people that knew that the LORD wanted them to stay, none of them lost anything and none of them died. The pastor said that when he prayed about it, the LORD showed him the story of Paul.

If we look at the story of Paul, we see that he was on a ship in a harbor. That harbor was considered "unsafe." It was labeled unsafe because it didn't have protection surrounding it. If bad weather came, the ship could be lost or at least heavily damaged. Paul had gotten a Word from the LORD and he told the captain of the ship that they needed to stay there even though a hurricane was coming. The captain did not listen. He proceeded to leave that harbor. He was heading for a "safe" harbor. The storm hit and the ship was not going to make it. When the captain finally followed Paul's advice, no one on the ship died. The ship was destroyed, though.

We need to seek the LORD's face about where our family should be. Remember, sometimes the answers that the LORD will give you will not make sense to conventional ways of thinking. Our family wants to live in Israel. That goes against any conventional way of thinking, but if that is where the LORD wants us to be, then that is the best place for us to be.

I trust that you will get the LORD's instructions on where to live and where to go. He will provide for you when He sends you.

"The fear of man bringeth a snare: but whoso putteth his trust in the LORD shall be safe" (Proverbs 29:25).

"The Name of the LORD is a strong tower: the righteous runneth unto it, and is safe" (Proverbs 18:10).

Matthew 10:28 says, "And fear not them which kill the body, but are not able to kill the soul: but rather fear him which is able to destroy both soul and body in hell."

BEAR ONE ANOTHER'S BURDENS

When we moved out of the mobile home, one of our friends asked me when we were going to buy a washer and dryer. I told her I didn't know. She told me that she believed we should have them since we had four children. I told her that it wasn't a necessity; there were Laundromats everywhere. I told her that I had to make sure other things were taken care of first. I told her that I believed God was calling her to carry that to the LORD in prayer. I believe that is what the scriptures tell us to do. We are supposed to carry one another's burdens. It is much easier to carry someone else's burdens than to carry our own.

If we spend all of our time praying for our needs, it is easy to get our eyes off of God and what He wants us to do. We are responsible for seeking God and His righteousness first, and then He will take care of the rest (Matthew 6:33).

I ask you to seriously look around you and see what other people need. Also look to see if there are friends that you can partner with to carry each other's burdens. Remember, if all we do is pray for ourselves, it leads to being self centered and frustrated. God did not intend for us to live that way. Yes, we are supposed to pray for our families, but we are not to dwell exclusively on them.

When we intercede for others, we can "reap what we sow." If we don't pray for anyone but ourselves, then we don't have anything to "reap" from. Also, it is actually really depressing to hear ourselves repeat our problems over and over again. I have worked in customer service for many years. The one thing they teach you about dealing with someone who is upset is to listen carefully to what they have to say. They then tell you that if you have to refer them to a supervisor, you should be the one who tells the supervisor what is wrong. You see, if the customer has to repeat their story over and over again, they just get more upset. I will discuss how the LORD showed me how to pray later in this book.

When the LORD provided us a used, really nice washer and dryer set, I called my friend and thanked her. She asked me why I was thanking her. I told her that the washer and dryer had just arrived. She was thrilled. I thanked her for being the one to carry that for me. It was so much easier for me not to worry about that but to let her pray. Now she can reap what she sowed into my life.

I have a friend that has suffered through many things in her life. I took eight weeks out of my summer last year and I fasted and spent time every day praying for her. Great things have started happening for her. Now, I can reap what I sowed into her life.

"Bear ye one another's burdens, and so fulfill the law of Christ" (Galatians 6:2).

"Beareth all things, believeth all things, hopeth all things, endureth all things" (1 Corinthians 13:7).

It is a great experience to learn about carrying other people's burdens. God loves it when we do that. It will also develop strong bonds of friendship between you and the other person. I intercede for them. They intercede for me. It is as simple as that. We feel better, and we keep the LORD's blessings flowing. The miracles start happening and continue to happen.

1 Corinthians 13 is known as the love chapter. It is saying that love bears, believes, hopes, and endures. We need to be willing to bear, believe and hope with our friends and family. We need to be there to carry their needs to the LORD in prayer. By doing that, we are helping them to endure their times of struggle and challenges.

MY "MINNESOTA CONNECTION"

This chapter is dedicated to all the intercessors who have helped save countless lives over the years—in prayer—that may never know what good they have done until they get to heaven. A person may never thank you personally, but God will some day.

I had a lot of headaches, especially during allergy season. I would take medicine and then usually end up with a sore throat. The doctor I worked for said that he had noticed a pattern to the sore throats. He believed I was having an allergic reaction to aspirin.

I had a sore throat, but this time was different; my throat was badly swollen, and I had the signs of strep throat. I went to see my doctor. He said that I had one of the worst cases of strep throat he had ever seen. He gave me a shot of penicillin and some prescription-strength aspirin. I told him that the doctor I worked for said I should not take the aspirin. This doctor told me that it was "impossible" for me to have a sore throat as an allergic reaction to aspirin. He sent me home.

Well, I got worse. By this time, the doctor's office was closed. I didn't realize just how bad it was until it was too late. I remember lying on the sofa, propped up at an angle so that I didn't have to swallow. I realized that I was close to death. When I tried to say something to my husband, I found that I couldn't speak.

I remember staring at the clock and thinking, "I'm going to die." I was thinking, "God, you told me that you were going to take me to the promised land. I didn't know that you meant heaven!" It was 8:30 p.m. My husband was watching TV. He was sitting in the recliner next to the sofa.

At 8:35 p.m., my husband jumped up and came over to the sofa. He picked me up and put me in the recliner. He went and got a bowl of ice water and two washcloths. He dipped the washcloths in the ice water and put one on my forehead and another one on my throat. I jumped because it was ice cold and I had a 103-degree temperature. He said to me, "If you want to live, we must do this." I felt a strange sensation in my throat and on my face.

At 8:38 p.m., I found that I could speak again, and I said to Joe that all the swelling in my throat was gone, but my face hurt. Joe came over and took me over to a mirror. I had hives all over my face and neck. But, thank God, I could speak and swallow. It was later proven that I had had an allergic reaction to both the penicillin and the aspirin.

The next day, the doctor gave me a shot of Benadryl to help the allergic reaction, and it made hives spread all over my body. It turns out I was allergic to that also. A couple of days later, I called my friend Miriam in Minnesota. I told her that I had almost died on Saturday night. She told me that she already knew that. She asked me to tell her what happened at 7:30 p.m. her time, 8:30 p.m. my time. I told her that I had realized at that time that I couldn't swallow and that I was going to die. She told me that she was in a meeting at church when God spoke to her and said, "Debbie is dying! Intercede!" She left the sanctuary and went to the nearest classroom. She laid herself down prostrate before the LORD and started praying. She asked me what happened at 8:38 p.m. I told her that was when I realized that my throat was fine. The hives had moved from my throat to my face. She said that made sense, because the LORD spoke to her at 7:38 p.m. her time and told her "It is done. You can go back now." She got up and went back to her meeting.

By the way, the doctors cannot explain why the ice-cold washcloths worked. Joe only knows that God told him to do that and to do it right then. God works in mysterious ways.

ANOTHER TESTIMONY OF PROVISION

My husband knew that I was feeding our family of six on forty dollars a week. I had been doing that for years. I had to do that because that is what our budget allowed. We needed to pay our other bills. A few things happened that helped him to appreciate what I had done.

One day, we were going by a grocery store. He said we needed cereal, so we pulled into the parking lot and parked. I gave him four coupons for cereal that I had in my purse. He told me he didn't want them. I told him to just put them into his pocket to humor me. He reluctantly agreed. He came out about ten minutes later. He had two boxes of cereal, both of which were ones I had given him coupons for. I asked him what happened. He said, "Have you seen the price of cereal lately?" I had to laugh. He didn't bother me about the coupons anymore.

One day, he saw them announce on a TV program that they were going to have an expert on the next day who was going to tell you how to feed your family of six on fifty dollars a week. He told me that he wanted the entire family to watch the program with him. The next day, the lady came on and showed what she feeds her family "on fifty dollars a week." My husband and children were appalled at the weird stuff she was making her family eat. After that, my husband stopped complaining for good. In fact, he would compliment me all the time and thank me for the meals. It was great medicine for the entire family. You can trust the LORD to help you feed your family no matter what budget you have.

DEATH PART 1

I have a friend who was diagnosed with breast cancer several years ago. She would be fine, and then there would be times that she would struggle with her faith. It is certainly understandable, but that is when you need friends to help encourage you. Her husband was in denial about her cancer, so he wasn't any help. He had told her that she wouldn't be sick unless she was in sin. Of course, that isn't true. Her pastor came to visit her one day a couple of days before her surgery, and he told her, "Don't worry; some people actually do live through this." What a terrible thing to say to her. She called me and was extremely upset. So I told her that I was coming over to her house to pray with her. I told my husband what was going on, and he said that I should definitely go. I got in the car and started praying.

The LORD spoke to me in the car on the way to her house. He told me that he lets people have choices from time to time on whether they want to go to heaven to be with Him or if they want to stay on earth for a while longer. He said that Sarah was experiencing this. She would be fine, and then the spirit of death would come "knocking," and she would freak out. He told me what she needed to say to end this.

When I arrived at Sarah's house, I told her what the LORD had told me. I told her that all she needed to do was to repeat these words: "I, Sarah, do hereby speak to Death. I declare that I will live every day that God has ordained for me to live. I will not die a moment early or a moment late. Death, you can't have me." Much to my dismay, Sarah then said that she wanted to go be with the LORD. I was in shock, and I thought about it for a moment. I then asked her if she was prepared for her children to be raised by her husband alone or by her husband and a new wife. She thought about it for a moment. She then said that she knew she had to stay, so she repeated these words after me:

> In the name of Jesus, I declare that I will
> live every day that God has ordained for me
> to live. I will not die a moment early or a
> moment late, but only at my appointed time.
> Death, you cannot have me.

Remember, our prayers are not supposed to manipulate God. *Our prayers are supposed to give God the control.* This prayer does that. The other great thing about this prayer is that it covers everything: accidents, crime, terrorism, illness, and everything else.

Immediately the fear subsided, and she never experienced it again. She came through surgery great. She recovered extremely well. In fact, she ended up in better health after the cancer was gone than she had been in before the whole thing happened. She even looked healthier. I am happy to say that Sarah is still alive and doing well today.

DEATH PART 2

I was flying to see my sister in Spokane, Washington. I have flown many times. I do not have any fear of flying, but as I was leaving work to pick my family up so that my husband could take me to the airport, something was bothering me. Strange things were going through my head, things like, "Be sure to tell your family that you love them." I rebuked the spirit of fear, since that is the first thing to come against. The feelings just wouldn't end. When I went to the airport, I still couldn't shake the feeling. There was increased security at the airport (this was the year of the Atlanta Olympics), but I still felt strange. When I got on the plane in Florida, I was sitting next to a nutritionist, so I was relaxed and having a great conversation with him. Soon, I started feeling uneasy. I decided to take what I had experienced with Sarah's situation and pray. I prayed the following: "In the name of Jesus, I will live every day that God has ordained for me to live. I will not die a moment too early or a moment too late. I rebuke you, Death. You cannot have me." I felt an immediate calmness, so I didn't worry or concern myself with it anymore.

I actually had a great conversation with the nutritionist about my husband's health. He was telling me exactly what my husband needed for his problem with his liver. We will talk more about that in the next chapter.

When I got to Atlanta, I ate dinner at the airport and then proceeded to the next gate. It was announced that there had been a problem with our airplane and that there was going to be a delay while they pulled another plane out of the hangar. Later on, we found out that one of the doors on the plane wouldn't seal shut. We were delayed approximately twenty minutes. I immediately thought that that was the problem I had felt the uneasiness about.

I got on the new plane, and the plane proceeded to the end of the runway. We were sitting at the end of the runway, waiting for our turn to take off. All of a sudden, our plane started up and took a sharp turn. It took us back to the terminal rather quickly. We were rushed out of the plane. The plane was then rushed away. The airline security personnel ushered us into a large room and then locked us in. It was really strange. We had no idea what was going on. The only thing they would tell us was that there was another problem. They brought us food and drinks. After a couple of hours, they ushered us into buses, and we were taken outside of town to a large field. They had people in swat gear around the field. They also had what appeared to be large panels of bulletproof glass between the swat members and the luggage. They sent us out into the field a couple of people at a time. We were told that we had to identify our luggage. We had to carry our luggage over to a swat member, and they would mark it. After this was done, they took us back to the airport.

Finally, they got us all on the plane. It was late. We had spent several hours in Atlanta. When I arrived in Salt Lake City, I found out that I had missed all of the planes going into Spokane for the day. They told me the fastest way to get to Spokane was to fly to Seattle and spend another five hours in the airport there. The next morning, I would then fly from Seattle to Spokane. The airline supposedly made the arrangements for the change in plans.

As I was walking to the other gate in the Salt Lake City airport for the Seattle flight, one of the employees for the airlines told me that security had found a bomb in the luggage on the plane in Atlanta. He said that the terrorist had called when we were at the end of the runway and said that he was blowing up the plane. I guess the terrorist didn't realize that it had been delayed. The man then told me about three other flights they had found bombs on that week. He said the planes were flying out of Alaska, Los Angeles, and Connecticut.

When I went to get off the plane in Seattle, I thought I was going to have to spend the night in the terminal. I immediately went into the restroom. When I came out, the terminal was totally empty. A security guard came along and told me that I had to leave that terminal because it was closed for the night. As I was going through the security area at the end of the terminal, one of the security guards asked me if I was okay. He said that I looked really tired. I told him that I had been delayed in Atlanta for several hours and that I was going to have to spend the night in the airport there. The other security guard asked me the number of the flight that I had been on. I told her. She slapped the other security guard on the arm and told him that he should be nice to me since I had been on an airplane that had a bomb on it. She then proceeded to tell me that they had found bombs on three other flights that week. She said that the planes were flying out of Alaska, Los Angeles, and Connecticut.

The female security guard felt bad for me, so she took me to the "Mother and Babies room." It was locked and had a private bathroom and a sofa for me to lie down on. It also had a pay phone (this was before I had a cell phone), so I called my family and let them know what was going on. I then lay down and slept for a while. The security guards would come and check on me every hour. It was really helpful to finally get some rest and to be secure. I really appreciated the security guards' kindness.

The next morning, I got up and went to the ticket counter for the commuter airlines that I was taking to Spokane. They said that they had not gotten a reservation for me. They asked me if I was okay. They said that I looked really tired. I explained to them everything that had happened to me. The lady then asked me if I had been on flight X. I told her yes. She asked me if I knew that they had found a bomb in the luggage on that flight. I told her yes. She also told me that they had found a bomb in three other planes that week: one from Alaska, one from Los Angeles, and one from Connecticut. She made a phone call to the other airline and got it worked out. I got on the plane to Spokane. While on the commuter plane, a flight attendant noticed that I was tired. I told her about my delay and she told me the same thing about the bombs in the other planes.

When I got to Spokane, my luggage was missing. So, I had to file a claim. An attendant at luggage claim told me the same exact story.

I enjoyed my visit to Spokane, and I returned safely to Florida. I do believe that there are a lot more things caught by security than is ever allowed to go public; otherwise, there would be a panic, and no one would fly at all. I do not believe that all of the airport and airline personnel would have told me the same story with the same locations if it had not been true. Try the "phone game" sometime. You can't get that many people to get the same information if you tried, especially in three different cities. The only logical place out of the three is Los Angeles. I do not think that you would just naturally think that there would be bombs on planes in Alaska and Connecticut.

I prayed and asked the LORD why I went through that whole experience. He showed me that He wanted me to know what it felt like to get a warning from Him in my spirit about a dangerous situation. I do plan on living in Israel, so that makes perfect sense.

FEAR VS. FAITH

One of the important lessons that I learned over the years is that fear activates the enemy, and faith activates God. There is a healthy respect that we have for things in nature, such as not reaching out to touch a rattlesnake or walking up to a bear. That is not what fear is. One of the definitions of the word *fear* is "to expect with alarm" or "to expect the worst." The word *faith* means "trust in God; firm belief in something for which there is no proof."

At one point in my life, I let fear get a grip on me. I would get up and check the locks on the doors several times before I could go to sleep. I would also double check the locks on the windows. One night, I was getting up to check the locks again, and I heard the LORD speak to me. He said, "What you fear will come upon you." I knew what He was talking about. Job 3:25 says, "For the thing which I greatly feared is come upon me, and that which I was afraid of is come unto me." That is a key verse to the entire story of Job. Do you let fear keep you from enjoying your life? Job ended up getting the thing that he feared the most. He is clearly an example of someone that allowed fear to get a grip in his life and look what happened.

There is one thing that I learned to do. If I feel an overwhelming fear coming on me, I simply pray, "I rebuke the spirit of fear in the Name of Jesus." If I still feel a concern after that, I then pray over the situation. In this way, if it is an attack of fear from the enemy, you stop it. If it is a warning from the LORD to pray, then you also take care of that by praying.

Examine your heart and ask the LORD to reveal to you any hidden fears that you have. Ephesians 4:27 tells us, "Neither give place to the devil." So, we cannot keep these things hidden. We must clear them out of our lives.

"… nothing shall by any means hurt you" (Luke 10:19b).

"For we walk by faith, not by sight" (2 Corinthians 5:7).

"… the just shall live by faith" (Galatians 3:11b).

"For therein is the righteousness of God revealed *from faith to faith*: as it is written, *The just shall live by faith*" (Romans 1:17).

In Matthew 9:29, Jesus said to a man, "According to your faith be it unto you." Luke 5:20 tells us that when the LORD saw a man's faith, the man's sins were forgiven. Romans 14:23 tells us that whatever is not done in faith is sin.

The only exception to the rule of faith activating God and fear activating the enemy is that we are to have a healthy fear of the LORD. The definition of *fear* that applies here is "to have a reverential awe for." That is because God is holy and He is the Almighty One. We need to respect His power and righteousness.

"The fear of the LORD is the beginning of knowledge: but fools despise wisdom and instruction" (Proverbs 1:7).

"The fear of the LORD is the beginning of wisdom: and the knowledge of the holy is understanding" (Proverbs 9:10).

"The fear of the LORD is the beginning of wisdom: a good understanding have all they that do His commandments: His praise endureth forever" (Psalm 111:10).

We need to be sure that the only fear in our lives is the fear of the LORD. If we understood the righteousness and holiness of God, we would be concerned about offending and hurting Him. I grew up with a healthy respect for my earthly father. I knew not to talk disrespectfully about him or to him. We are supposed to live our lives like that with God as well. In fact, God deserves even higher respect than that. When I did something to disappoint my father, I would see it in his eyes. If only we could see God's eyes when we do things that we know will hurt Him. We should be living a lifestyle and a way of life that aims towards the mark of not disappointing the God of the universe.

He sent His son to be sacrificed on the cross for our sins. Why would anyone want to abuse that sacrifice? The Bible teaches us that we must be committed to living a life totally dedicated to Him and that we must not put anything before Him. When we submit our desires to Him, we are showing our respect for Him and His sacrifice.

NATURAL HEALING

I have learned something over the years. God heals in many different ways. He heals through doctors. He heals through divine intervention and prayer. He heals through the laying on of hands and anointing. He also heals through natural means.

My husband worked a job where he didn't get any paid sick time. We didn't have money for him to miss work, so he would work through his sicknesses. He drove trucks delivering doors, usually alone, so he wasn't exposing other people to being sick like you would in the food or customer-service industry. He would take a lot of

medications when he had colds or the flu. He didn't realize that he was taking too much acetaminophen. After a
while, my husband felt achy and lousy most of the time.

Joe was a regular blood donor. Finally, a notice came
to us from the blood bank stating that his LFTs (liver
function tests) were really bad. When he called the blood
bank, they told him that his LFTs had been off for quite
a while, but that they don't notify the person until tests
come back bad the third time.

When Joe went to his primary care doctor (that I was
working for at the time) and asked about this, the doctor told him that it meant Joe was an alcoholic or had
been sleeping around and had picked up hepatitis. My
husband was extremely upset. He doesn't drink, and he
doesn't sleep around. So my husband went to the library
and started investigating the situation. That is when he
found out that acetaminophen is extremely toxic to the
liver. He came home and read the labels more thoroughly
on the cold medicines that he had been taking, and he
soon realized that he had taken too much.

It turns out that the symptoms of acetaminophen-
induced liver damage are:

1. headaches

2. weakness

3. aches and pains

Why do you take acetaminophen? For those exact things.
That is why people can end up dying. If the liver damage

isn't caught early enough, they would need a liver transplant or it would be fatal.

He went back to the doctor and told him, "My LFTs are off because I have suffered liver damage from taking too much acetaminophen."

The doctor then said to my husband, "Darn, I keep forgetting about that." The doctor then called some other patients he had been struggling to find an answer for, who also had bad LFTs. He asked each one of them if they took acetaminophen. Each one of the patients answered yes and admitted that they took it all the time. He told them all to stop immediately. He then got appointments set up for each patient to see a specialist. The doctor also wanted Joe to see a specialist.

In the meantime, I had started praying about what to do. In church the next Sunday, there was a time during the service when the pastor asked everyone to get into groups of three to four and pray for each other. This lady turned around and asked us what we needed prayer for. I told her that Joe's liver functions were off and that we had determined that it was from acetaminophen-induced liver damage. She told us, "Oh, Joe, you need to go on milk thistle and COq10."

It was only a week later that I was on the plane going to Spokane. Remember, I said that I was on the plane next to a nutritionist. I asked him about what Joe should do. He told me that Joe should take milk thistle and COq10, as well as a certain amount of vitamins C, E, A, etc. I was really excited to have a confirmation about that.

I went to the health store when I returned from Spokane. They had a small library there. I researched it and found out how much Joe needed to take of each thing. I bought most of the vitamins at other stores by watching for sales and using coupons. I put together a vitamin "cocktail" for him to take every day. He didn't like taking all of the pills that I was giving him.

He started taking the vitamins, but he still went to the specialist. The specialist told him that there was medication that he could give him that would fix his liver, but it would destroy something else in Joe's body. He told my husband that what he really needed to do was to go to the library, do research, and put together a vitamin "cocktail" to take that included milk thistle and COq10. My husband told him that I had already done that. The doctor sent him home, telling him that he needed to do what I had told him to do and take his vitamins. I had my confirmations (lady at church, nutritionist in the airplane, research into the subject, and a physician). It was great. I do appreciate it when doctors and nutritionists agree. Joe took his vitamins, and his liver has been fine ever since. That was almost twenty years ago.

DIVINE MEDICAL INTERVENTION

My husband had been severely injured on his job. His employer had sent him to their workers' compensation doctor, and he had refused to treat him for his symptoms. Since I had worked for doctors, I called them and asked them about that doctor. They had all told me that he was incompetent. They told us what his symptoms meant and what needed to be treated, but they were not orthopedic doctors, so they couldn't treat him. They all recommended that my husband see the same doctor.

Workers' Compensation was refusing to cover Joe's injuries because the employer was denying the claim. So we contacted our health insurance carrier. They said they would cover a doctor's appointment for a second opinion. They paid for my husband to see the orthopedic doctor that we wanted. This doctor was great. He knew exactly what was wrong. The only problem was the fact that he wasn't an in-network provider for our HMO insurance. Also, the insurance was saying they wouldn't pay for any more visits because it was a workers' comp injury. Workers' Comp was refusing to cover it, since Joe's employer was denying the claim. So we appeared to be trapped.

My daughter Julie was taking out the trash one day. A piece of glass came through the plastic bag and cut her leg. We had to take her to the hospital for stitches. A few months later, our insurance company called from their home office. They asked me how she had cut her leg. I explained it to her. She said that it was okay and that they would pay the hospital bill. She asked me if everything was okay. I told her no. I told her that my husband was on the verge of having permanent nerve damage in his neck because workers' comp was denying the claim and the insurance company was refusing to pay for him to get the care he needed due to the fact that he was injured on the job. She said that she could "fix" that problem for me. She said that she had the connections necessary to get his neck and arm injuries covered. Within two weeks, the insurance company notified me that they would cover the claim. Now, we just needed to find the right doctors to treat my husband.

A few days later, on a Sunday night, the great doctor that we had really liked called us. He asked my husband how he was doing and why he hadn't been back to see him. This doctor is a well-known hand and arm orthopedic specialist in South Florida. It was absolutely amazing to us that he cared enough to call. We told him that our insurance company wasn't letting us see him because he wasn't on our list of in-network providers. He asked us what insurance we were on. He told us that he would join our plan and that his friend, a highly renowned neck specialist in Florida, would also join our plan to take care of Joe's neck. We had heard of him from news stories about him putting a famous singer back together after an accident and helping her to walk again when she had been told that she wouldn't be able to walk. He said that Joe better hurry. Since we had terrible insurance, he and his friend were only going to join the plan for six months in order to take care of Joe. It was amazing. Joe ended up having two of the best orthopedic doctors in the country do his surgeries instead of the terrible workers' compensation doctor he had been sent to. We are not saying that all workers' comp doctors are bad, just the one Joe was sent to.

It all came together just because Julie cut her leg taking out the trash. It was all totally God. Joe had a disc in his neck that was blown into small pieces, so it had to be removed from his neck, and a bone from his hip was put in. He also had to have surgery on one arm and get therapy for the other arm.

Sometimes God expects us to walk through the medical experiences, but when we do, we certainly should pray to have the very best of care. I truly believe that it is a miracle that this doctor cared so much about Joe that he would follow up with him. There are still great doctors in this world. Praise God for them.

DIVINE PROVISION/ INTERVENTION

When my husband was out with his workers' comp injuries, we didn't have his income to help us. His employer was denying everything. In fact, his employer at the time even told us that they were going to "bleed us dry." They told us they knew we had four children and that they were going to make sure they held out on us until we gave in and dropped the whole thing. We knew this wasn't right.

We decided to believe God for our provision and take a stand for the truth and what is right.

God provided for us in some spectacular ways. We had friends who would just show up on our driveway and give us money. We would use that money for rent. I was working part time, and I would pay our other bills with that. I tried working full time, but it wasn't working. Joe was on too many medications at the time, and I had to care for him and the children. We tried to get food stamps, but the food stamp office said that I would have to quit my job (which I had been working at for several years) and get a full-time job. They did let us have food stamps for two and a half months. Our church helped us out twice, but they had a policy that they will not help you more than that. They paid our rent once and our electric bill once. We did appreciate their help.

Joe had worked with a man who loved to fish, but he didn't want to clean them or eat them. So, he would call us and say he had a bucket of fish for us, and we would go and pick it up. It would be a large painter's bucket full. My children and I would filet them. My father-in-law was concerned about us eating so much fish. He sent us an article about the mercury levels in fish. We pointed out to him that the last paragraph in the article said that the safest fish in the world to eat was a fish called "Nile Perch." It absorbs no mercury. It turns out that the only kind of fish that Joe's coworker was catching was "Nile Perch." God was feeding us the best.

One of the grocery stores in the area decided to start supplying boxes of fruits and vegetables to our church to help people in need. Someone on staff at the church that knew about our situation would call us when the boxes arrived and we would go to the church to pick up the food. They also would box up anything they had left from the bakery or deli. Once in a while, we would get a ham or chicken from the deli thrown in, but we mostly got vegetables and fruit. We might end up with eight to ten crates of bruised vegetables and fruit. I was giving food every week to several single mothers I knew. I also had a coworker whose husband was out of work on injuries. It was a complicated situation that took several years for the insurance companies involved to straighten out. I would take them food every week.

We started getting huge bags of bagels. In one week, they gave us 450 bagels. We couldn't possibly eat them all. We took out what we could eat. The single mothers got what they could use. My coworker got what her family could use. My kids took the rest of the bagels out into the neighborhood with grocery bags and let the neighbors pick out what they wanted. The neighbors knew about my husband being out of work, and it was quite a testimony to the neighbors that we were feeding them.

We sat down to dinner one night and paused to pray. Suddenly, I cracked up laughing. I couldn't help it. Soon, everyone was laughing. We were looking at the "multiplication of the loaves and the fishes."

One day, my husband came to me and told me that he understood our finances but that he was frustrated with the cheap deodorants I had been buying. He really missed his favorite deodorant. There was one particular kind he really liked. I told him that he needed to pray about it.

The next week, I went and picked up the crates of vegetables and fruit. I was sorting through a box of fruit when I was surprised by something sitting in the middle of the oranges. I called my husband over. I said, "Joe, did you pray for that deodorant that you wanted?"

He said, "Yes."

I said, "I can tell. Come over here and see this." You guessed it. Sitting in the middle of the oranges was the very kind of deodorant he wanted in the very scent he wanted. I will never forget that day. I still laugh about that. God even cares about the little things.

We never ate as well as we did when Joe was out of work. God doesn't provide junk. When He provides, He provides the best. With His help, we made it through three and a half years without Joe's income. We never went hungry. We still had everything. We had not been evicted, and we still had our two nice used cars. We did not lose a thing.

Psalms 50:14–15 says, "Offer unto God thanksgiving, and pay thy vows unto the most High: And call upon Me in the day of trouble: I will deliver thee, and thou shalt glorify me."

SUPERNATURAL PROTECTION

I had a friend who was married to a very abusive man. He would spank the children with a board, and he would break and throw away any toys that were out when he came home from work. He would remove a part of her car so that she could not go anywhere. He would make out a schedule for Carol every day, and then he would stop by the house to check to see if she was "on schedule." She and her children were being terrorized. I told her she needed to divorce him, but other people in the church were telling her that she could not get divorced unless she had proof that he had committed adultery.

I got really frustrated, so I decided to call and get some prayer over the situation. I called a national ministry that had a prayer line. It turned out that they were having a call in that day. Instead of a prayer counselor, I ended up getting to speak to the head of the ministry on the air. He asked me if the woman's husband had been approached by men of God about his problems at least three times by people who she had not spoken with—in other words, men of God who had heard from the LORD about the situation. I told him that there had been three men of God who had approached him. He told me that I should tell Carol to divorce her husband and to instruct her to tell her husband the following: "I am not divorcing you for my sake. I am divorcing you in order to step out of the way so that the LORD can correct you. As long as I stay, you will not feel the need to change." I told her that, and that gave her the courage to divorce him.

When she filed for divorce, he threatened to kill her, so we knew we had to cover her and her children with prayer. They lived in a large, old home. Carol knew that he owned a couple of guns and that he had them hidden in the house, but she had not been able to find them. She didn't have the money to move, so she continued to live in the home while waiting for the divorce to become final.

One day, I was busy making dinner. I felt an irrepressible urge to call her. My children were pestering me for dinner, but I could not get rid of the feeling that I had, so I picked up the phone and called her. She could hear the kids asking for food to eat, and she could hear the clamoring of the pans and dishes, so she asked me why I was calling during such a busy time of day while trying to make dinner. I told her that I didn't know, but that I had felt the urge to call her. Suddenly I heard a loud noise, and she yelled at me, "He's breaking in, please pray." The phone then went quiet; she had hung up to call the police. The door was locked, but her ex-husband was breaking in.

I called my friend Shirley, and we started praying. After twenty minutes of praying, Shirley said that she felt that it was over and it was all okay. Later that evening, Carol called me, crying. She said that her husband had broken through the locked door and was standing in the entranceway. He couldn't move his feet. He started screaming that something was holding his feet down and that he couldn't move. It took the police twenty minutes to get there. In the meantime, he was standing in the entranceway, saying, "Why can't I move my feet?" He couldn't move until the police arrived. At the moment the police arrived at the door, his feet were released to move. Carol just knew that I was praying. But it was the power of agreement between Shirley, myself, *and God.*

He never attempted to kill her again. He knew he better not try. The police didn't arrest him. They said that since the lock wasn't broken, she couldn't prove that he broke in. That did not make any sense to me, but we knew that God was in control. Also, a few months later, she was at the gym working out, and a woman next to her started to talk about the "great" guy she had been seeing for several years. When Carol questioned her about the man, it turned out that it was her husband. So, she had proof of adultery after all.

> Great is our LORD, and of great power: his understanding is infinite. The LORD lifteth up the meek: He casteth the wicked down to the ground. Sing unto the LORD with Thanksgiving; sing praise upon the harp unto our God.
>
> Psalm 147:5–7

PRAYER THAT CHANGES THINGS

"Cast thy burden upon the Lord, and He shall sustain thee: He shall *never* suffer the righteous to be moved." (Psalm 55:22)

There was a period in my life when the amount of prayer requests and the severity of the prayer requests were overwhelming. There were several cases of suspected child molestation among the people that we knew. There were several cases of cancer and other major illnesses that needed healing. I even had a case of a neighbor (who wasn't a Christian) who came to me at the pool one day. She told me that she had been told that I get answers to prayers and that she really needed help. She was extremely upset. Her mother, who had been disabled, had died. She had "fallen" down the stairs. She truly believed that her stepfather had pushed her mother down the stairs. The stairs led to the basement, and this woman knew that her mother didn't go near the stairs because she knew that it was dangerous for her to go near them. She certainly never would open the door to the basement, since she walked with a walker and was unstable on her feet. I told her I would pray.

I went to my room that night to pray, and I was extremely upset. The weight of all of the prayers was overwhelming. The other thing that bothered me was the uncertainty of everything. I didn't know if the man had killed his wife. I didn't know if the people that I knew were molesting their children. It was terrible. Finally, the LORD spoke to me. He asked me, "Isn't My burden for you supposed to be light?" I knew the answer was yes. That night, He taught me several important lessons about prayer:

1.   He told me to pray Him into the situations. He told me to pray His names into the situ-

ations. So, I first grouped all of the prayer requests into several groups. The first group needed healing. The second group needed deliverance from bondages like alcoholism, drugs, and pornography. The third group was for the suspected child molesters and murderers.

2. He told me to sing a song to Him with the prayer requests in it. (You don't have to sing, but it is good to try. Remember, you are alone, and He already knows what your voice sounds like.) Believe me, it relieves stress.

3. He also told me to pray for the truth to be made known in all of the situations. He showed me many scriptures talking about truth. Psalms 100 tells us that His truth endures to all generations. John 14:6 says that Jesus is *the way, the truth*, and *the life*. All three of these titles for Jesus are important.

4. He also told me to thank Him as I prayed. There are many scriptures having to do with thanking Him. I list several later on in this chapter.

This is how I would pray. I am leaving a blank where the names would go, but you know to add people's names in the blanks.

Lord God, I thank You that You are

_____ 's

Healer. I thank You that You are

_____ 's

Deliverer and that the truth will be made
known about their health. In Jesus' name.

He sent His word, and healed them, and
delivered them from their destructions. Oh
that men would praise the Lord for His
goodness, and for His wonderful works to
the children of men! And let them sacrifice
the sacrifices of thanksgiving, and declare
His works with rejoicing.

Psalms 107:20–22

For the people in bondage to things:

Lord God, I thank You that You are

_____ 's

Deliverer, Redeemer, and Savior. Lord
God, I thank You that You will go to the
gates of hell and back but that You will not
let them go. In Jesus' Name.

For the suspected molestation and killing:

Lord God, I thank You that You are the
way, the truth, and the life. I thank You that
You will make the truth known in

and in their family. In Jesus' name.

Since the situations regarding the molestation and murder were really serious, I decided that every time I stopped at the stop sign on this one corner at the edge of my neighborhood, I would pause and just say this quick prayer:

> LORD God, I thank You that the Holy
> Spirit will come down and the truth will be
> made known regarding
>
> _____ ,
>
> _____ ,
>
> _____ ,
> and _____ .

I would stop at this stop sign on the average six to eight times a day. It would only take a few seconds to pray the prayer, but it was being prayed all the time.

This way of praying was incredible. It made me feel good. It was easy *and* I got incredible answers to prayer.

Sometimes I would use a song that I already knew, but I would just adjust the words to turn it into prayer for people. This is an example:

> "Our God is an awesome God, He reigns
> over Julie and Jenny, He reigns over David
> and Jess. Our God is an awesome God."

> Speaking to yourselves in psalms, hymns and
> spiritual songs, singing and making melody in
> your heart to the LORD; Giving thanks always

for all things unto God and the Father in the name of our LORD Jesus Christ; Submitting yourselves to one another in the fear of God.

Ephesians 5:19–21

I will praise the Name of God with a song, and will magnify Him with thanksgiving. This also shall please the LORD better than an ox or bullock that hath horns or hoofs. The humble shall see this, and be glad: and your heart shall live that *seek God.*

Psalm 69:30–32

Let us come before His presence with thanksgiving, and make a joyful noise unto Him with psalms.

Psalm 95:2

Enter into His gates with thanksgiving, and into His courts with praise: be thankful unto Him, and bless His Name.

Psalm 100:4

Sing unto the LORD with thanksgiving; sing praise upon the harp unto our God.

Psalm 147:7

It really is easy to do. Try it. It's great. Take any song you like and see if you can adapt the words.

I soon realized that this way of praying was not only powerful, but it fulfilled several important principles/scriptures in the Bible.

1. First Chronicles 23:30 says that we are to thank and praise the LORD in the morning and in the evening.

2. Psalm 92:1–2 says, "It is a good thing to give thanks to the LORD, and to sing praises unto thy name, O most high. To shew forth thy lovingkindness in the morning, and thy faithfulness every night."

3. Second Chronicles 5:13 shows us that when we praise and thank the LORD in music, the glory of the LORD will come down.

4. John 8 tells us that knowing the truth will set us free. John 16 tells us in verse 13 that when the Holy Spirit comes, He guides us into all truth. Therefore, we can pray, and the Holy Spirit will come down upon a situation, and the truth will be revealed.

The answers that I got in the first six months alone were as follows:

1. Two people were healed of the illnesses they were diagnosed with, but one of the two people had gotten a new doctor that told her she was on the wrong treatment. As soon as

the doctor changed her treatment, she got well.

2. Another person needing healing was healed but only after they found out that she had been misdiagnosed. When they found the correct diagnosis, she recovered quickly. That is why the truth needed to be made known.

3. One man who was accused of molesting his children was found innocent. The truth about his wife came out. She had been seduced by another man, who convinced her to accuse her husband of molesting her children so that she could divorce him and get full custody of the children. The father ended up with full custody.

4. In another case of suspected child molestation, it was proven that it was someone in the family doing the molesting, but it wasn't at all the person who was suspected. It was someone that had totally "looked" innocent.

5. In another case, the daughter of a woman went to the police station. She told the police that she was tired of seeing her mother molest her stepsons. She had just turned eighteen, and she felt that the police might take her seriously since she was an adult. It was proven in court that the boys had been molested. The boys were taken out of her care.

6. I had been praying over the situation regarding the stepfather possibly killing his wife for six months. The stepfather went to the police station and told the police, "I haven't been able to eat or sleep for the past six months. I have to confess, I killed my wife!" It didn't have to go to court or anything. He went to prison. He confessed everything. The daughter came to me crying and telling me how relieved she was. She was so glad that she didn't have to go through a trial.

The beauty of praying this way is that you *are* praying the will of the Father. It is so easy to try to manipulate things through prayer. God doesn't want us doing that. That is why a lot of our prayers are not answered. Sometimes, we are just simply praying the wrong things. When we pray Him into the situation, we are releasing His power into people's lives, and He can and will do miraculous things *His way*. His way is always better than ours. Remember, "Lord, Your will be done: not mine." It is hard to let go and let God, but we do need to do that.

When we pray this way, He can take care of people in unique ways, because He is their *provider*. He can heal people in whatever way He chooses, because He is their *healer*. He can deliver people in whatever way He chooses, because

He is their *deliverer*. The right people will be found guilty, and the innocent will be set free, because He is the *Truth*. I truly hope that you find the true joy and simplicity to praying this way. It is amazing to see what God does when we cooperate. Don't fight His will, agree with it. The Bible teaches us to pray. He revealed to me that the most powerful way to pray is by releasing Him and His power into the situation. We will get more results praying this way.

Sometimes when we are not getting answers to our prayers, it is because the LORD knows something that we don't. There may be repercussions to things happening that we have not thought about. Sarah did not know what trouble would come out of her giving Haggar to her husband Abraham to sleep with. Sarah didn't seek the LORD about doing that. She took matters into her own hands. The LORD let her make her own mistakes. He will let us make mistakes because He created us to have choices. We also have choices on how to pray. We need to make the right choices. Why waste our time praying in a way that is not in agreement with His plans? It ends up just robbing us of our time and energy and not doing any good.

We will get more answers when we are in agreement with Him. In the "Testing For Endurance" chapter, I prayed and confessed repeatedly, but it didn't work because it was not God's will for me. When we don't pray in agreement with Him, we are wasting our time and energy.

Since then, I have also added pleading the Blood of Jesus over my family. I pray, "Jesus, I plead the Blood of Jesus over _____ ."
I pray this daily over every member of my family.

Psalm 145:18 says, "The LORD is nigh unto all them that call upon Him, to all that call upon Him in truth."

The LORD also took us through an interesting experience while we were staying at a friend's house. We had moved out of Florida, but we had not yet found a place to settle down.

There were some strange people that would hang out in the neighborhood we were living in. Guys would sit around in vans for long periods of time. It appeared that there were some things going on in the neighborhood that may not be the best. It made us feel uncomfortable. So my husband and I decided to march around the property and pray over it.

We marched around the property line and prayed, "We pray protection over this property, and we pray that Your angels will protect everyone on this property from physical harm. In Jesus' name, Amen." That night, someone managed to come in the front door of the house and turn the heat on and set the thermostat to 105 degrees. I had heard a noise during the night that sounded like the front door opening (the lock didn't work very well on it) twice, but I didn't hear any other noises, so I had gone back to sleep. We woke up an hour or so later. It was so hot in the house that it felt like a sauna. It was July, and the house we were staying in didn't have any air conditioning. I noticed that it sounded like the heat was on, so I went to check the thermostat, and I was stunned. I turned off the heat, and we had to open all the windows and turn on all of the fans that we had.

I prayed and asked the Lord, "I don't understand why this happened, Lord; we prayed over the property." He spoke to me and said, "You got exactly what you prayed for. No one was harmed, and the property wasn't damaged." I realized then that we do at times have to be specific. We then marched around the property and prayed this prayer: "Lord God, we place angels around this property. We put a hedge of protection around this property, and no member of the enemy's forces can cross this line: not criminal, civil, military, supernatural, or otherwise."

When we marched around the property, we also included the parking area in the street that was right in front of the house. At that moment, all of the pranks that were being played on our cars and the house stopped. So there are times when you do have to be specific.

We all need to take a day off from asking the Lord for anything from time to time. We need to just take a couple of days a month and just praise and worship the Lord. I raised four children, and there were days that I got so frustrated with them because they were constantly badgering me for one thing after another. Sometimes, I just wanted a day off from being bombarded with requests. So, take a day off once in a while and just take time to thank Him for all that He is in your life.

"Bless the Lord, O my soul, and forget not all His benefits" (Psalm 103:2).

"Blessed be the Lord, who daily loadeth us with benefits, even the God of our salvation. Selah" (Psalm 68:19). *Selah* means to take a moment to pause and think about it.

GOD CARES ABOUT EDUCATION

When we moved out of Florida, we found that our children's educations had been terrible. The average class size in the county that we lived in was forty-two students per classroom. The way that they got around the federal regulations regarding this was to have the children change classrooms every two hours. It didn't fix their education, but it did keep the school doors open.

We were traveling around the country ministering, and we weren't living anywhere in particular, so I was homeschooling. We decided that my oldest daughter was ready to graduate. She had taken the practice test and had passed it easily. She had scored in the 98th percentile. So I called the GED office in that state. They sent me papers that would have to be filled out in Florida and then be sent back. I knew that I probably wouldn't see the papers again if I sent them there. For one thing, three hurricanes had hit that area. I decided to call the GED office again. I got a different person this time at the GED office. She identified herself as Gloria.

Gloria told me that I needed to call this man near where I lived. She gave me his name and phone number. He is in charge of continuing education for this area. I called him. I told him the situation, and he told me that he would help her get her diploma. He asked me how I got his name and phone number. I told him that the GED office had given it to me. He asked me the name of the person there that I had spoken with. I told him "Gloria." He told me that there wasn't anyone there by that name. In fact, he said these exact words to me, "There is no Gloria there. Are you sure?" I told him yes. He then said, "Who knows? Maybe you spoke to an angel." I told him that I actually believed that it was an angel. He got really quiet. I think he was joking, but I was serious. He got my daughter tested, and she had her diploma four months early. She has since graduated from a Bible college.

My second child wasn't as easy. She had really pushed her education. She would even study and do extra work on the computer schooling program that we had, but she was definitely from a different planet when it came to math. In fact, she wasn't just from a different planet; she was from a different galaxy. I called Mr. Fields again. I explained to him that she was ready for graduation, but that she needed help that I couldn't give her with her math. He gave me the name of a tutor that does tutoring free of charge.

I took my daughter to meet the tutor. He gave her sixteen pages of math to do. We returned to see him a couple of days later. He went over the work, and there wasn't one single right answer on the sixteen pages—*not one*. He turned to her and said, "I see how you are thinking. I am going to fine tune your thinking a little bit, and I will have you ready for graduation in two weeks." I was shocked.

My daughter had always felt like she was stupid because she had so much trouble with math. He not only had her ready for graduation, but he also managed to get through to her that she was normal. He told her that it was totally normal to struggle with math. He told her that it is the subject that almost everyone struggles with. He encouraged her by taking her through a practice test and showing her how smart she really was. (She had really high scores in all of the other subjects, especially science.) I had been trying to tell her that, but she didn't believe me. She believed him though.

He not only had her ready, but he had her tested in two week's time. She had her diploma within a month. She graduated a year and a half early. He truly was a gift from God to us. She got a full scholarship to a major university. She has since graduated from there.

I didn't waste any time. I took my son next to see the tutor. He helped him get ready for his diploma testing. He was definitely smart enough to have graduated much sooner than he did, but he just didn't want to. He only graduated six months early.

My youngest daughter graduated as soon as the state would let her graduate. In fact, she was mad because the state wouldn't let her graduate until she was sixteen. She felt that the state was holding her back. It was tough waiting for her to graduate. She had taken a practice test at the age of thirteen and passed. She has now been in college for several years. She went to Israel a couple of years ago on a medical volunteer program. She spent two months there working in a nursing home. She loved it. In fact, she wants to transfer to Israel and finish her college education there. After that, she wants to travel with medical teams around the world to help the less fortunate.

I am so happy that educating my children for me is over. It was tough, but it was worth it. My oldest two children got accepted and have both graduated from college without having to take SATs or ACTs. All they needed to know was that they were home schooled and that they had high scores on their GED tests.

By the way, the man who was in charge of home schooling for the area called me. He told me that there was no way I was going to get diplomas for my children without going through him and without getting tested first myself to see if I qualified as a home-school teacher. I told him that it was too late and that everything was taken care of. He asked me how I managed that. I told him what Mr. Fields had done. He told me that he didn't know that things could be done that way. He asked me to forgive him for yelling at me and said that he wanted to know what he could do to make it up to me. I told him that he could make it easier for other people to come into the state who are good American citizens and who need to get diplomas for their children. He promised me that he would do that. Since I started getting my children their diplomas, they changed the forms, and they have made it easier for people. I am sure that there are many people who will benefit from the changes made.

We also need to be educated. We need to study the Word of God. I learned what I believe from the Word. My earthly father taught me that you are not supposed to go to the Word of God to back up what you want to believe or what you have been taught. We are supposed to study the Word of God to find out what to believe. There is a huge difference. I challenge you to start reading the Bible over again. This time, take the time each day to pray over your time and ask the LORD to open the Word up to you and show you what you need to get out of it. He will show you things that you have never seen before. The Word will come alive.

"The heart of the prudent getteth knowledge; and the ear of the wise seeketh knowledge" (Proverbs 18:15). *Prudent* means "marked by wisdom."

"For wisdom is a defense, and money is a defense: but the *excellency of knowledge* is that wisdom giveth life to them that have it" (Ecclesiastes 7:12).

MY UNRAVELING

I have been injured by many people over the years. Most of them have been people in authority over me, such as pastors, teachers, etc. It happened everywhere we went. I got more and more frustrated over the years. I ended up a mess. I didn't feel like I could trust anyone in authority over me anymore. I will spare you the details. I know that many of you have been through the same thing. I know that many of you feel like I did. I decided that I should trust no one.

I know what the Bible says about people that hurt you. Matthew 5:44 says, "But I say unto you, love your enemies, bless them that curse you, do good to them that hate you and pray for them which despitefully use you, and persecute you." God obviously thought that this was important, because He repeated this again in Luke 6:28. Luke says, "Bless them that curse you, and *pray for them* which despitefully use you," so I know that it is an important part of forgiveness to pray for the people who hurt you. I have a personal policy of putting anyone that does something to seriously hurt me on my daily prayer list for at least two years. I will keep them on longer if the LORD tells me to. I do want to clarify my statement, "something to seriously hurt me." If someone looks at me the wrong way or doesn't say hi to me, that should not even be considered as something that hurts you. Something that hurts you is something done that is specifically and intentionally an attack on you or your character.

I didn't want to pray for the people that hurt me. The LORD kept telling me to, and I kept saying that I couldn't. Finally, the LORD asked me, "How do you feel when you think about X?" I told Him how upset I was with that person. He asked me, "Do you want to see that person spend eternity in hell for what he did to you?"

I said, "No, but it would be nice if he could visit there for a day or two!" It sounds funny now, but I was totally serious.

Well, the LORD told me, "I can deal with that." So, He told me to start out praying that the person would repent for what they did so they would not have to be judged for that later and that they would learn from the mistakes they had made. At the same time, I would ask the LORD to help me to forgive them. It felt great. As I prayed for the person daily, I found that my attitude improved. I was actually praying for that person's redemption. There is no greater thing that you can pray for someone. I eventually would find myself praying blessings over the person. It was great. I knew that through this, I had done all that I needed to do in order to forgive them. This is important, since the Bible is very clear about the importance of forgiveness. After all, it is the enemy's plan to keep us in unforgiveness in order to destroy us. Matthew 18 tells us that we must forgive in order for our sins to be forgiven.

When we moved to our current location, we decided to try out a new church. When we went there, we were really impressed with the sermon. We are firm believers in the fact that pastors should preach the Word. We are tired of hearing people get in the pulpit and talk. Ministers should be teachers of the Word. Anyway, we ended up deciding to stay for a while and see what would happen. The pastor and his wife seemed genuinely nice, but I still had my guard up.

One day, I dropped my husband off at work and was on my way to the YMCA to work out, and the LORD spoke to me and said, "You can trust Scott and Donna." Scott and Donna were the names of our pastor and his wife. I started to cry. I pulled out my cell phone and called Donna. I told her what the LORD had said to me.

She responded by saying, "Of course you can trust me, but why would He need to tell you that?" I dumped all of my past hurts on her.

When I got done, she told me that she had no idea why anyone would treat me that way. I was shocked because I

had become thoroughly convinced that there had to be a
flaw in me that attracted that type of treatment. She reassured me on how much she and Scott loved me and my
family. In fact, she told me all of the great qualities that
she saw in me and my family. I was shocked. Well, that
was the beginning of a new work in my life.

They opened up the entire church to letting us do
things. We did every Jewish feast and festival with the
church. The children's pastor opened up the children's
church to me. I taught the children all of the feasts. I then
started teaching when the children's pastors needed time
off. I found myself opening back up.

I became hyperemotional again. I went to the doctor
and had my blood pressure and blood sugar tested, and
everything was fine. We weren't sure exactly what was going
on. My husband, son, and I went to a conference, and there
was a woman there who had come over to meet us. She
had invited us over to her house. She was really nice. My
husband and son went to a museum during the afternoon
break from the meetings, and I went to spend the afternoon
with my new friend. We had a long talk about our lives.
She told me that she sensed unforgiveness in me. I told her
that it wasn't unforgiveness. I had already dealt with that in
my life. I told her that what she was sensing was actually
open wounds. I had finally figured out what was going on. I
explained to her what had happened. Every time someone
hurt me, I would apply another bandage. Well, I had been
hurt so many times that I was a walking mummy.

Because I had been so bound by my bandages, my per-
ceptions of things around me were off, and I got injured

more that way. The bandages also caused other people to perceive me wrong too. It was a vicious cycle of injury after injury. She told me that she thought that if you were a mature enough believer, you wouldn't get hurt. I told her, "Even if you are a mature enough believer, you will still get hurt. Let's say, if a person comes up to you and punches you in the eye, and you are a mature believer and you reach out and hug them and tell them that it is okay, you will still have a black eye." She told me that she didn't agree with that. I told her that if I was right that the LORD would confirm it to her. That night, we went back to the conference, and her pastor got up to introduce the speaker. He said that he was going to be ministering on a very special topic the next day. He said that the LORD had told him that there are many people in his church that cannot trust him or his wife because they had been injured repeatedly by people in authority over them. The LORD told him that even if you are a mature believer, you would still end up with an injury. The LORD gave him the same illustration about being punched in the eye as I had given that woman earlier that afternoon, so I knew I was on to something. The woman was amazed at how the LORD confirmed this so quickly.

What the LORD did for me through Scott and Donna was incredible. They provided me love and acceptance. That is what I needed so that I could let the LORD take my bandages off, one by one. They won't admit it, but I know that it must have taken some prayer on their part to love me during that time in my life. Scott and Donna have since moved on to another church in another city, but what they did for me personally will always be with me.

God wasn't done with me yet. I had been praying for years to lose weight. I had tried different diets, and I would lose some weight and then get under some stress and put it back on. I needed more than a diet. I had been working out at the YMCA six days a week for a long time, and that didn't help me to lose weight. I got stronger, but not thinner. Sarah (from Death Part 1) knew how frustrated I was, so she offered me a home to stay in that she and her husband were fixing up and trying to sell. One of my daughters was getting married in August, so I planned my trip for the fall. In the meantime, I searched for a plan to go on that was different from the usual diets.

I ended up going on a plan that was designed by the son of the chiropractor (from Chapter 4). I had a six-week "sabbatical." I worked out for three hours a day, and I would spend on the average six hours a day with the LORD. I had my prayer list with over three hundred names on it that I prayed over every day, and I had two other prayers that the LORD told me to pray each day. I lost a substantial amount of weight. In fact, I am continuing to lose weight.

The first prayer that I prayed is this:

> In Jesus' name, I cancel any negative words anyone has spoken about my health. I cancel any negative words I have spoken about my health or about anybody's health. I speak

life and health to my body by the power and dominion given to me by God almighty. I speak forgiveness. I forgive anyone that has harmed me or any member of my family. I forgive myself for any and all mistakes that I have made. I set myself and the other people free in the name of Jesus. I pray the prayer that Jesus prayed, since there isn't anyone sick in heaven. I say that God's will be done on earth and in my body as it is in heaven. I speak to my body now; be healed and be made whole in the name of Jesus. Amen.

God personally gave me the following prayer to pray when I was praying over my healing and over my trip.

Dear heavenly Father,

I thank You, LORD, that Your Word tells me in Matthew 7:7–8, "Ask and it shall be given you; seek and ye shall find; knock and it shall be opened unto you; for every one that asketh receiveth; and he that seeketh findeth and to him that knocketh it shall be opened." I have asked, so I shall receive my miracles; I have sought You, so I shall find You; and because I have knocked, the doors shall be opened to me. Jeremiah 30:17 says, "For I will restore health unto thee and I will heal thee of thy wounds, saith the LORD." I thank You, LORD, that You are restoring my health and healing all wounds. Matthew

21:22 says, "And all things, whatsoever ye shall ask in prayer, believing, ye shall receive." I thank You, LORD, that because I have asked in prayer believing, I am receiving the victory. Psalms 147:3 says, "He healeth the broken in heart and bindeth up their wounds." I thank You, LORD, that You are healing my heart and binding up all wounds. Psalms 37:5 says, "Commit thy way unto the LORD; trust all in Him and He shall bring it to pass." I have committed my ways to You, and I trust in You. I know that You are bringing the answer to pass. Psalms 84:11 says, "For the LORD God is a sun and shield: the LORD will give grace and glory; no good thing will He withhold from them that walk uprightly." I thank You, LORD, that You are my sun and shield and that You are pouring grace and glory down on me and that You are withholding no good thing from me because I walk uprightly. Isaiah 54:17 says, "No weapon formed against thee shall prosper; and every tongue that shall rise against thee in judgment thou shalt condemn. This is the heritage of the servants of the LORD, and their righteousness is of me, saith the LORD." I thank You, LORD, that no weapon formed against me shall prosper, and every tongue that rises against me in judgment will be stopped and that You are helping me to stop those tongues. Romans 10:11 says, "For the Scripture saith, whosoever believeth on Him shall not be ashamed." I thank You, LORD, that You are taking away all shame, and I won't be ashamed anymore. I thank You, LORD, that You are taking away all pain and shame and You are replacing it with Your glory and grace! I thank You, LORD, that this plan that I am following isn't just following principles. It is for me to be *empowered to fulfill my purpose and calling.* In Jesus' Name, Amen.

Please note that in the prayers, you do not call any illness or wounds "mine" or "my." The wounds are no longer mine. Jesus took them from me, and He will take them from you.

I know that there are other people in this world that have been hurt like I had been. My prayer is that your healing has started while reading this book. I challenge you to pray the two prayers I have given you and ask the LORD to "unravel" you. I also pray that you will find a place to worship where you will be safe. No place on earth will ever be perfect, but you can be in a place where you are loved unconditionally and can feel the LORD's love.

It is easier to just cover the injuries over and try to forget about them, but that isn't healthy for you. You need to trust the LORD that He will heal those things in your life. It is part of submitting to Him. Remember, it wasn't Him that hurt you. There are a lot of people that run around saying things in His Name, but that doesn't mean that it is from Him. I want you to ask the LORD to put people in your life that you *can* trust. The LORD brought Donna into my life, and He will bring someone into your life that you will be able to trust with your darkest hurts and secrets. But the first person that you need to be honest with is yourself. The second person is God. After that, He will direct your path. We cannot move forward while holding onto the past. We have to let the past go. Sometimes we can't see what is ahead of us and that keeps us from stepping out. That is because the LORD is preparing us to step out in faith. After you take the step of faith into the unknown, the LORD will meet you there. Let this verse from Jeremiah be our prayer: "Heal me, O LORD, and I shall be healed; save me, and I shall be saved: for thou art my praise" (Jeremiah 17:14).

Seek the LORD's face and ask Him to show you what you really are. I know that God has called my husband and I to move to Israel, so that is where I will be the very best that I can be. The enemy works overtime to try to convince us that we are not worth anything. Do not believe his lies.

Now that you have started to see yourself through the eyes of the LORD, I am asking you to make a list of the people that have hurt you by telling you over and over again that you were "worthless" or something else negative. I had people in my life that kept doing that, but I have moved on. But when I first started on my path of healing, I had to do this. Once you have made the list, I want you to do the following:

1. See that person that has hurt you as a hurting person. They would not have acted that way unless they were wounded themselves. One of my favorite sayings that I use to remind me to be merciful is "they didn't get messed up by themselves. They had help." What this means is that there are things that happened to that person that helped make them act that way.

2. Add them to your daily prayer list if you haven't already done so. Be nice now. When you pray for them, you can start out by simply praying for them to be healed of their internal injuries so that they will not hurt anyone else.

3. If the person has passed away, then you can pray for the family members that they have left behind.

HE IS
OUR FATHER

It is a good thing when we have respect for our natural father, but it is even more important that we have a healthy respect (fear) of God. He is a righteous, holy God, and He won't be mocked. If I made fun of my father when I was growing up, I knew that within seconds, I would experience the correction/discipline for acting that way, but we do not hesitate to use God's name in vain or to talk disrespectfully about Him. We are to live our lives in a respectful manner. I have a wonderful natural father. I know that I do not want to disappoint him in any way. I could see the disappointment in his eyes if I did something wrong. I endeavored not to have that happen very often. We should actively seek out a lifestyle and a way of life that does not disappoint the God of the universe. After all, He is a righteous God.

> The fear of the LORD is the instruction of wisdom; and before honour is humility.
>
> Proverbs 15:33

> He will fulfill the desire of them that fear Him: He also will hear their cry, and will save them.
>
> Psalm 145:19

> By *humility* and the *fear of the* LORD are riches, and honour, and life.
>
> Proverbs 22:4

Please note: *Humility and the fear of the* LORD *are what God calls "riches."* It is the total opposite of what the world is trying to make us believe.

Psalms 95:1–7 tells us to:

1. Sing to Him
2. Thank Him
3. Place Him above all things
4. Worship Him and kneel before Him
5. Believe that we are His sheep

As His sheep, we are to take time to hear His voice and follow His leadership. Sheep don't ask questions. They just follow the shepherd's voice. If they don't follow the shepherd's calling, tragedy can strike them very quickly. We need to understand that our ultimate protection depends on our learning to listen to His voice and to obey it quickly. We need to follow His instructions for our daily lives. We need to take time to hear His voice and follow it. We need to accept His wisdom. We need to heed to His instructions.

> And when He putteth forth His own sheep,
> He goeth before them, and the sheep follow
> Him: for they know His voice.
>
> John 10:4

> As a shepherd seeketh out his flock in the day that he is among his sheep that are scattered; so will I seek out my sheep, and will deliver them out of all places where they have been scattered in the cloudy and dark day.
>
> Ezekiel 34:12

> I am the good shepherd, and know my sheep, and am known of mine.
>
> John 10:14

> My sheep hear My voice, and I know them, and they follow Me.
>
> John 10:27

> For ye were as sheep going astray; but are
> now returned unto the Shepherd and Bishop
> of your souls.
>
> 1 Peter 2:25

God is our Father. If a father just hands everything over to his children as soon as they ask or even before they ask, we say that he is "spoiling" them. Yet, we think that God should do that for us. Just like a child growing up, God gives us more responsibilities as we develop and mature in our walk with Him. I know what it feels like to be a parent and have my children demanding things from me. I know what it feels like to be treated like I am only loved for what I give them. It feels terrible. Why do we think that God doesn't feel the same way? When He gave His only begotten Son, wasn't that enough?

I have a friend that kept begging God for a certain type of car. He didn't really ask God if that was what he was supposed to have. I only heard him saying that it was what he had to have. Finally, he ended up with it. It was the worst car. It was in the repair shop *twenty-eight times in the first year.* The transmission even blew at 50,000 miles. It was still under warranty, but the family was on the way home from a vacation at the time, and it caused trouble for them having to pay the deductible (I think it was $100) and having to get transportation home and then back again to pick the car up. I know that God knew he shouldn't have that car, but he kept "claiming" it. He would have been better off submitting his will to God and letting God lead him to the car that he should have.

We are *not* God's boss. Sometimes we treat Him that way. My children want things all the time that they shouldn't have. They are adults now, and I certainly can't stop them. They have a choice. Things still work better most of the time if they ask us or ask someone with knowledge about the item they want to get. We need to ask God. He knows everything anyway. He is the expert in everything. There isn't anything He doesn't understand.

We need to understand that the LORD has the benefit of knowing what is coming. He then knows what needs to happen and what we need to learn in order to get through what is coming. This is part of totally trusting Him. It is essential that we let Him have His way.

God is not rude. He is not going to barge into our lives. He comes in when we invite Him to come in. He made us to have a free will.

I truly believe we need to submit everything to Him. Ask Him for creativity in your daily life. He will show you how to grocery shop, what to buy, how to cook, how to be a better parent, how to be a better spouse, how to be a better employee and get a better job, and how to spend your money. Life is exciting when you are submitted to Him. There isn't one single miracle that happened in our family that I would trade away. Life is an adventure. Let God be the guide. Submit to Him. He will make your life a beautiful adventure too.

Psalm 37:3–5 says,

> Trust in the LORD, and do good; so shalt
> thou dwell in the land, and verily thou shalt
> be fed. Delight thyself also in the LORD; and
> He shall give thee the desires of thine heart.
> Commit thy way unto the LORD; trust also
> in Him, and he shall bring it to pass.

This scripture clearly outlines what we must do in our life.

1. You must *trust* the LORD.
2. You must *delight* yourself in the LORD before
    you can expect Him to give you the desires
    of your heart.
3. You must *commit* your way to the LORD. You
    cannot choose to skip any of these things.

All of these things are part of *total surrender*. Hold nothing back. There is nothing like total surrender. How can you truly be born again if you are holding back part of yourself? To be born again involves all of you! Have you ever known of only a partial birth of a baby? No, of course not. Why do we think that our lives are going to be blessed by the LORD when we are holding back? There are partial-birth abortions, but that is to kill a baby. Don't let God's plan for you be aborted. We have no reason not to trust the LORD with *everything*. Remember, His plan is for good, not evil. How do you experience all that He has for you? By submitting your entire life to Him, desires included.

LORD, I thank you for everyone who has read this book. I thank you that the Word that has been planted in their lives will not return void. I thank you that the Word will bear fruit in their hearts and lives. Please lead each person that has read this book to a place of healing in their lives. Help them to stay on the path that leads to life. LORD, please guard each person's heart as they go through the healing process. In Jesus' name, Amen.

Be blessed in the name of the LORD.

The LORD bless thee, and keep thee: The LORD make His face shine upon thee, and be gracious unto thee: The LORD lift up His countenance upon thee, and give thee peace.

Numbers 6:24–26

Amen